101 Ways to Practice Purpose in Your Life

The Art of Being

Dennis Merritt Jones

Foreword by Michael Beckwith

New Reality Press

For information:
New Reality Press
P.O. Box 940837
Simi Valley, CA. 93094-0837
www.DennisMerrittJones.com

Printed in the United States of America

Library of Congress Cataloging-in-Publication Data

Jones, Dennis (Dennis Merritt)
The art of being: 101 ways to practice purpose in your life / by Jones, Dennis Merritt.
   The art of being : 101 ways to practice purpose in your life / Dennis Merritt Jones.
     p. cm..
   Includes bibliographical references.
   ISBN 0-9746414-0-5

   1. Spiritual life. 2. Spiritual exercises. 3. New Thought.   I. Title.

   BF639.J66 2003   299'.93
                           QBI03-700836

Cover design: Michelle Lee Kenney
Cover art: Evelyn Jones
Back cover photo: Michael Downey
Editor: Kim Robinson
Interior design: John Shaw

Contents

The Art of Being

DEDICATION

It is from the depth of an unfathomable love and great respect that I dedicate this book to my best friend, Diane. She happens by no mistake to also be my wife, my lover, my spiritual playmate, my cheerleader, and most importantly, my partner in life. By her example, she has taught me the sweetness of extending selfless service and loving-kindness to others, whether friends or strangers. This planet is a better place because of her presence here. Truly, God has blessed me beyond measure with the gift of this lady in my life, whom I will love forever.

ACKNOWLEDGMENTS

Seldom is an author blessed with a team of individuals who make the creation and publication of a book easier or more fulfilling than those I have had the privilege to work with on this project. From the onset, when this book was but a vision, it has been blessed by a number of people who have gone so far beyond the call of duty that I find myself truly humbled by their generosity of spirit, time, talent, and loving-kindness.

First and foremost, I want to express my gratitude to my editor and friend Kim Robinson, whose ability to see the potential of this book has turned it into a living, breathing reality that will add something life affirming to all who read it. Kim's gentle spirit, blended with her uncompromising integrity to keep the words true to the purpose of this book, shines through on every page. Kim not only edited this book, but she also shepherded me through the maze of production and publication rituals necessary, while helping to keep me focused on the higher reason for sharing these ideas with the world. Kim has been a true friend and mentor, and I give great thanks for having her in my life. In the same light, I extend my gratitude to John Shaw and Michelle Lee for their creative vision and execution of the design elements and layout concepts for this book, which also includes the brilliant cover design.

To my spiritual community, the congregation of the Simi Valley Center for Positive Living, I say Namaste, and I thank them for being a vast source of inspiration from which I drew in the course of writing this book. Their presence in my life has encouraged me; it has helped me help others by means of these writings, which originated as a way to daily connect with those in my own spiritual community via email. Soon thereafter, I had the opportunity to redefine what "spiritual community" meant, because as my daily messages quickly spread, people all around the world became part of my spiritual family. And so, to those thousands who are part of my extended, global, spiritual community by virtue of my daily email, I also offer my deepest thanks for their love and support. Their willingness to share with me their personal victories and stories of the peaks and valleys encountered while exploring the terrain of life, discovering who they have come here to be, is proof that there is something powerful and good within each of us that is simply waiting for us to awaken to Its presence and rise to the call.

To my friend Patrick Harbula, I say thanks for introducing me to Kim Robinson. To Gary Peattie at DeVorss Publishing, I offer my gratitude for his encouragement and generous advice along the way. To my spiritual brother Mark Johnson, I say thanks for the gift of time at his spiritual retreat in Hawai'i—it was there that this book came to be a completed idea in spirit. To Ernest Holmes, Michael Beckwith, Mary Manin Morrissey, Walter Starcke, Gary Zukav, Don Miguel Ruiz, Frank Richelieu, Cherie Carter-Scott, William Curtiss, James Golden, Fletcher Harding, and all of the other amazing beings who have inspired, encouraged, lifted, prodded, motivated, befriended, and loved me enough that I could become the vessel by means of this book, I thank them for being there. Their wisdom has been the hand of God I have held so tightly. I also wish to acknowledge every individual whom I quote in this book; it started with them, they have been my daily companions and my heroes. Truly, I give thanks for each one, for without them, this book wouldn't be. To my parents, Russ and Evelyn Jones, I offer thanks for being available as the vessels through which my life took form in 1949. They have been exquisite teachers of how to love the whole of life—I'm glad I picked them. I also wish to acknowledge and thank my mother for allowing me to use her beautiful painting that graces that cover of this book. Her original artwork is a perfect example of the beauty to be found in being who we have come here to be.

Finally, with true humility, I acknowledge the real author of this book. I offer this book as a living testimony to what is possible when one makes space in his or her life for spirit's love to manifest. This book is a labor of that love. And so, it is with a deep reverence for all life, and the greatest of respect for you, the reader, that I acknowledge the source of it all—God.

Peace,
Dennis Merritt Jones, D.D.

FOREWORD

There is a haunting call within our consciousness enticing us toward reality. Reverberating within our soul, it urges us to become and express increasingly more of our essential self. We are on the planet to respond to that call, to wrap our consciousness around the divine treasure within us, and to be joy, creativity, peace, compassion, and unconditional love. Each and every one of us is an individualized expression of undivided reality.

In his spiritual classic, *The Science of Mind*, Dr. Ernest Holmes wrote, "Never was there a cosmic famine. We may stumble, but always there is that Eternal Voice, forever whispering within our ear, that thing which causes the eternal quest, that thing which forever sings and sings."

With its mountains, deserts, valleys, and oceanic vastness, confident footing and balance is required for navigating the terrain leading to that which sings and sings within us. And, because at times we tend be a little hard of cosmic hearing, the singing may not necessarily sound so sweet. Eventually—despite years of cleverly dodging and postponing—there comes that mystical moment when it's as though an audible voice shouts through the clouds of our density, "You there . . . Yes, I mean you . . . You're busted—it's time to wake up!" Ah, the first step in humility: listening. This leads to the second step: surrendering. It's often at this juncture that one begins to seek a teacher and teaching that outstretches a hand of compassionate guidance for the journey to reality. Wise are those who firmly and humbly grasp that benevolent hand.

The transmission of spiritual awakening may wear many faces, but in truth, there is only one: that which is. Our universe is not a "was" or a "will be" system. It is an "is" system vibrating within the "now" measurement of time. This great is-ness custom designs itself for each one of us, perhaps in the form of a book, a temple, a teacher, a teaching, even a challenging experience—whatever it takes for us to begin answering the perennial question: "Who am I, and where am I going?" Simply put, our primordial purpose is to respond to the impulsion from within to solve the mystery of our individual existence, to find and be the authentic self that is, has been, and ever shall be.

Even in our current state of development, we are perfect candidates for awakening. At whatever juncture in our lives we pierce the illusory thought that we have a separate existence from that which is, the cosmic clock will be set at the only time it keeps: now. How patiently the awakened self vibrating and circulating its life force within us awaits our reacquaintance with the reality of who and what we really are.

"Who am I, and where am I going?" You are the answer to this question. You are here to ask the question and to be the answer. Using the very stuff of your everyday life is a potent place to begin a conscious experience of awakening. You can choose in every moment of each circumstance, each activity, spoken word, and thought. Stepping into the moment with an awakened mind removes the tension from making that choice. Wakefulness causes each moment to be fresh. We make each choice as though it's the first time, and we make it with utmost clarity and discernment of mind. Then we become cocreators of our life with its very source—that which simply is.

This is not to deny that our daily routine is filled with repetition from our morning rituals to getting our children to school on time, to our professional life, to praying and meditating. But each time we bring to those routine activities an awareness of "now," we raise our vibrational frequency and cause the freshness of the moment to fall upon us.

With disciplined practice, the mindful choices we make originate more and more from our innate intuitive faculty. This is beyond the conditioned mind that is so inundated with evidence provided by the five senses, which, though delightful, is limited at best.

We accelerate our path to awakening by choosing and practicing—with tools that function precisely—those techniques taught by the awakened beings of the world's wisdom traditions. Meditation and prayer have withstood the test of time. They work today as perfectly as they did for those who first practiced and perfected them. In fact, modern science stands in awe of the effectiveness of prayer and meditation. Today's advancements in quantum physics and experiments with prayer and meditation in medical laboratories are proving the efficacy of spiritual practice. By making a choice to meditate and pray each day, we sensitize our inherent faculty of intuition and begin to directly catch the cause and purpose of our lives. We mature into a spiritual understanding of how we are to be in the world. Wisdom-guided choices cause us to become a beneficial presence on the planet. Living in this vibrational frequency leads to inspiration and visionary thinking. Gratitude takes over our lives.

Right now, as you read these words, the call is upon you. It is nudging you. Love is nudging you right now. Compassion is seeking to come through your heart today. There is within you a soul, hungry to glow with the radiance of the awakened self. You and your choice-points-to-be merge to form the answer to your question: Who am I and where am I going?

Having chosen this book to read is a reasonable indicator that you are even now facing a moment of choice in your life. And you want your choice to be a conscious one, an enlightened one that will lead you out of the labyrinth of suffering whether it's mental, emotional, spiritual, existential, whatever the urgency and craving for relief. In life, there are no hiding places. No exits. Having run the gauntlet of hiding from life as it is, isn't it time to step out and surrender to the call, to be the life that is your authentic self and thereby express your authentic purpose on the planet?

In *The Art of Being*, Dr. Jones generously, gently, and powerfully offers the gifts of his own journey. He has taken the universal truths of the New Thought/Ancient Wisdom tradition of spirituality and shown their relevance to the challenges we face in twenty-first-century living. Most important, the spiritual brilliance of his own intimate experiences of waking up unfolds for the reader in a transformative understanding that inspires the soul into action. May this book be for you a special friend, an introduction to the power and presence of that which we call God, the very essence that invites you to be you.

Michael Beckwith, D.D.
Founder and Spiritual Director
Agape International Spiritual Center
Culver City, CA 90230
www.Agapelive.com

INTRODUCTION

I invite you to explore with me the idea that because you have been given the ultimate gift, the gift of life, you are already fulfilling your purpose on this planet, whether you know it or not. The important question to ask is, Are you are doing it consciously or unconsciously? Once awakened to the fact that you are already serving your purpose comes choice. You can choose to direct your energies and intentions in a manner that honors the giver of the gift of life, making your purpose and how you express it more rewarding and meaningful to you.

As you read, it won't take too long to discover that the intention of this book is to deepen your awareness of your spiritual nature. In short, it's about practical spirituality. The reality is that you can't be any more spiritual than you already are because you are 100% spirit. The challenge lies in living in an awareness that this is so. Spirituality is simply the art and practice of consciously being spiritual. Every human being's purpose is identical: It's to "be" the spirit of God manifesting in the human condition. As you awaken to being, your entire perspective of life changes. Some teachers have referred to this shift in perception as going from seeing yourself as a human being, stuck in the human condition, struggling to have a spiritual experience, to knowing you are a spiritual being, having a divinely human experience. That's why we are here—to become that conscious vessel through which heaven touches earth!

To help make this concept more vivid, imagine a time long ago before you were a physical being, when you were pure essence—no form, no personality, no name, no gender, no identity of your own, just one in the essence and allness of God. Now, imagine that God loved Itself so much and so fully desired to know and experience more of Its own divine Self, that from within Its creative nature, a form described as "you" is manifest and sent on a mission to earth.

At that moment, you became a soul being and understood your mission clearly. God said, "Go to the earth and be an individuation of Me." To complicate matters, however, the very last thing you heard from God as you departed on your mission was, "Oh, by the way, you won't remember any of this when you get there!"

So, here you are! Your true essence, the soul being that you are, is slipped into a garment of flesh and bone, which by now has had all kinds of labels slapped on it. In addition, you were blessed with a personality that has helped create and maintain the self-concept of who you think you are. Our soul recognizes who we really are and seeks to awaken us all to that divinity which seeks expression. You would not be reading this if it were not the case. This book is dedicated to assisting you in awakening to that presence within that knows its purpose and is simply seeking to be the divine expression of God in all that you say, think, and do. The amazing thing is that as you strive to consciously be who you have come here to be, life takes on a richer, deeper meaning than you ever dreamed possible. Your every action becomes a sacred act and a spiritual experience. So, it's not so much who you think you are on the earthly plane or even what you do, it's how you do it. It's the mindfulness in which you "do your life." That's what the art of being is all about!

There is no one right way to use this book. Each of the 101 individual writings can be used as a separate daily reading. A mindfulness practice is offered at the end of each writing that offers practical steps you can take to embody and more fully realize the ideas presented. I encourage you to take the time to do the work. It will help deepen your experience of being. Ultimately, the understanding at which you will arrive is that spirituality, the art of being, is actually a lifestyle. It's a way of walking our sacred earth every day.

I am pleased and honored that you have joined me on this mission and that we will travel together for a period of time. I am grateful for soul beings like you who are awakening to the reality that simply living every day with a sense of the sacred is to live a life of purpose. In doing so, everything you touch will be blessed by the love of the beloved, and ultimately, you will have done what you came to do, leaving this planet a better place than it was when you arrived. Know that in choosing to read this book, you will be deepening your skill in having an intentional and conscious spiritual relationship with God, life, and perhaps most important, yourself.

Know also that you are loved and blessed beyond measure.

Peace,
Dennis Merritt Jones, D.D.

1   WHAT GIFT DO I BRING?

As we explore the nature of our gift, our goal is to move toward this kind of giving: cheerful giving that flows gently and easily, kingly giving that flows surely from who we are. As we encounter the questions – Who are we? What do we love? – the gift we bring will be easy, because our gift naturally emerges from who we are. The offering we bring is ourselves, just as we are. Our gift is our true nature. There can be no greater gift than this.

~Wayne Muller

Can you remember the first birthday gift you were given? It was probably all neatly wrapped in a box with brightly colored paper and bound with bows (i.e., "stuff" to a kid) that seemed to take an eternity to remove before you could get to the goodies. Can you remember the delight you felt when you discovered the gift inside? Now, can you imagine yourself AS that gift? I believe each of us came into this human experience because we are on a divine assignment: to bring our gift to our Earth family. The gift we each bring is unique and unlike any other. It's a one-of-a-kind gift, which can never even in a million millennia be recreated. The challenge, however, can sometimes lie in figuring out how to get the gift opened! God was very creative in this endeavor because He wrapped this gift in an amazing package—your consciousness! It's true. The gift you have brought to share with your family of the earth lies in who you are. Who you are—or who you believe yourself to be—is the gift you bring. Can you feel the delight of this delicious truth? You are a gift to humankind and the planet, tightly wrapped and waiting to be opened.

Once we become conscious of the fact that we are on a mission to reveal this gift to the world, we might wonder where and how we begin to unwrap it. There is so much "stuff" to remove before we get to the gift itself! In many cases, I believe we already know what lies within the unwrapped gift of our being. We are just uncertain and fearful that if and when we do reveal it to the world, it may not be well received. Let's face it, there is nothing worse than giving a gift that isn't appreciated and welcomed, right? (That's one the "bows of belief" we need to remove.) So, we spend a good amount of our life looking at the wrapping that covers the gift, and we use the excuse that there's so much stuff wrapped around it that it would be easier to leave it unopened. Often, there is so much needless shame wrapped around the gift we are that we hold back on giving of our authentic self to anyone. This is why Wayne Muller encourages us to clarify who we are. We are defined by who we believe ourselves to be and by what we love. Who we are is no less than the sacred essence of God Itself. The question is, do we know this? Once we are aware of this truth, it automatically makes the gift that we are acceptable, just as it is. This awareness and acceptance leads us to take actions that bring us closer to what we love. In so doing, we begin sharing our gift with our family of the Earth. Don't hold back on giving what you have come to share. The gift of you really is quite unique, and that is what makes it one-derful.

Mindfulness Practice

- Take a few moments to contemplate the question, "What gifts do I bring to share with my Earth family?" Go within and take an emotional scan or inventory of all the qualities that make you who you are.

- Be sensitive to the feelings of joy and passion that will accompany any authentic gift you have come to share.

- Realize that the feeling you are experiencing is the divine essence of God within saying, "Yes, this is why you have come. This is your mission: to be the living vessel through which I may express and flow with grace, ease, and love."

- Today, commit to seeking new ways to open up the gift you are by sharing it with others. Realize, you are the gift God has given to Itself!

2

*Some believe all that their parents, tutors, and
kindred believe. They take their principles by
inheritance, and defend them as they would their
estates, because they are born heirs to them.*

~Alan W. Watts

Recently, I saw a bumper sticker that read: We All Live
Downstream. My first response was that it seemed an accurate
sentiment about life. It was, for me, another affirmation that what I do
in life will affect all of those who come after me. This is true on several
different levels. From an environmental perspective, how I treat this
planet becomes part of the legacy that I leave to my grandchildren's
grandchildren. From a spiritual perspective, how I treat my children
becomes part of my legacy to their children's children.

This point was brought home ever so clearly when my
seventeen-year-old daughter made her grand entrance, coming
down the stairs in her formal gown for her first prom night. Yes, I
was stunned by her maturity and beauty . . . my little girl, turned a
radiant young woman seemingly overnight. But what I really saw as I
cleared the tears from my eyes was the continuum of the stream of
life, flowing from her great grandparents, her grandparents, and
finally through her mother and me into her. She is the recipient of
the genes and consciousness of all her family members who came
before her. This was true from the moment she was born, and it will
be so as she brings her own children into this world, adding not only
her genes (and mine) to the mix but the accumulation of her beliefs
about life (and mine) . . . and so on it flows. I'm grateful that she
was born the same year I entered the ministry. If by no other means

than osmosis, she has been "marinating" in an awareness of God's presence in her life as her anchor since the day she arrived. It's obvious to me by the manner in which she lives and relates to others with reverence, selflessness, and unconditional love. So I rest well assured, knowing that those who live downstream from her will be very fortunate indeed.

The teacher Jesus was very clear on this downstream principle when he said, "The sins [mistakes] of the father [parents] are passed down to the son [children]." However, what he didn't point out is that the good character traits of the parents are passed down too. Having said this, I don't take too much of the credit for who my daughter turned out be, because frankly, there were more than a few mistakes made along the way. Given the chance, like most parents, I probably would do some things differently. I believe that her early exposure to spirituality as a lifestyle made the difference. She learned early on to define herself as a spiritual being having a human experience.

Life really is a stream into which we pour our beliefs, and all of those who come after us will be the direct beneficiaries of what we believe. The great thing is that with this awareness comes choice! As we awaken to the fact that we don't necessarily have to pass on beliefs that have not served us or others well, we can choose to eliminate them from the legacy we pass on. The real question is, who is it that lies downstream from you from this moment forward? It's never too late to change your legacy and gifts to future generations.

Mindfulness Practice

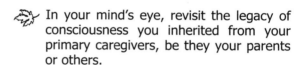 In your mind's eye, revisit the legacy of consciousness you inherited from your primary caregivers, be they your parents or others.

Have you been living from the beliefs given to you without questioning them? Do they serve you well and will you pass them on to others downstream? You may think that it's too late because "my children are already grown and with families of their own."

It is never too late to make a difference in someone's life. Reach out to your family in a way you may never have before. Volunteer for a mentor program. Become a youth church teacher. Spend time with young people. Find a place to be a living example of unconditional love, reverence, patience, and selflessness.

Live consciously aware that all of life is a sacred experience, and the legacy you leave will enrich others far downstream.

3

THE VIEW FROM THE FREEWAY ISN'T THAT GOOD

The heights charm us, but the steps do not; with the mountain in our view we love to walk the plains.

~Johann Wolfgang Von Goethe

There was once a large group of travelers who were seeking to enhance their view of the country in which they lived. They wished to know all of it more fully and the distant mountains called to them silently, promising them a view that would change their lives forever. They set out with excitement down the wide four-lane freeway in their comfortable motor homes heading toward the mountains. As they reached the foothills, the freeway ended and turned into a dirt road, which they followed until it became so narrow that their big comfortable motor homes could go no further, and so they set up camp. Yet there were those who wanted to go higher, knowing the view would be better and so also would be the reward, so they set out in their four-wheel-drive SUVs. Soon enough, they too could go no further as the path to the top became even more steep and narrow. But at least they could look back and see their friends and the valley below. So, although the view wasn't that great, they were content with it and set up camp. Then, those few who had trail bikes and yearned for yet a greater view rode up the path until it grew so narrow and steep that they too could go no further. They shouted and waved to all their friends below and settled for the limited view, which was very nice, but there was still something missing. Finally, one last traveler knew that if he could just hike the extremely narrow path and eventually climb the rocks for the last mile, his view would be unparalleled and magnificent and so too his reward. As he reached the top of the mountain and surveyed the entire country below, he felt sad for his friends, who by their own limited efforts had settled for less and would never know the awesome view he had attained through his persistence and commitment. Then, a deep inner peace swept through him as he had never known before, and of course, instantly his life was transformed and he lived happily ever after in eternal bliss!

The moral: It's true that the spiritual path does grow more and more narrow the further we move up the mountain of an evolved consciousness. It does become more challenging to stay on it. Many people truly desire to experience the view from the top, garnering the rewards of inner peace and transformation that come with it, yet few are willing to leave the motor home consciousness behind.

Practicing spirituality at the level of a motor home consciousness is not a discipline, it is a matter of convenience. When it becomes too much of an effort, we set up camp in the flatlands of consciousness and go no further. A freeway has many lanes to accommodate the hoards that are looking for instant spirituality (and instant gratification). As we evolve, the path narrows and there are fewer traveling companions because it requires a deep dedication and a willingness to explore the unknown. Of course, the ultimate view we all seek is a clear view of life through God's eyes. This is a journey into your own God consciousness. Hey, if it were easy, everyone would be walking around with deep, sincere smiles on their faces and a sense of wholeness, well-being, and inner peace that can only come from that divine place—at the top of the mountain within. Wouldn't that be nice? Seek the mountain today.

Mindfulness Practice

⟫ Do you consider yourself to be on a spiritual quest? Are you going as far up the mountain of God consciousness as you would like to go?

⟫ In the above analogy, what mode of transportation would you be using on your journey? A motor home, SUV, trail bike? Or are you walking up your own path of self-discovery?

⟫ What disciplines must you commit to and what instant gratifications must you let go of in order to reach the mountaintop?

⟫ Now, make a list of action steps you can take to get you to the next level of the mountain and do the work. The view is worth it and so are you!

4

IT'S NOT WHAT
YOU SAY

*There is brutality and there is honesty. There is no
such thing as brutal honesty.*

~Robert Anthony

The depth of any relationship is measured in part by the ability of those in the relationship to express themselves freely, saying whatever is on their minds. One of the qualities I have discovered and cherish most in my relationship with my wife Diane is our willingness to make it a safe place to communicate in absolute honesty. Honesty, which is an outward expression of integrity, is the foundation on which every solid relationship is built. Without honesty, there can be no trust, and without trust there can be no true inner peace for the people in the relationship. Likewise, if the people in the relationship are not at peace, the relationship itself will not be at peace. That kind of relationship will not be a happy or healthy place to hang out.

What I have noticed is that there is a dance of energy that happens as Diane and I enter into that sacred space of saying what's on our minds. It requires great mindfulness on both our parts to say "what needs saying" in a manner that will be received by the other with an open mind. What we have both discovered is that it's not what you say but how you say it that matters most. If we take the time to get in touch with the emotional charge (energy) that lies behind our thoughts before they become words, putting ourselves in the other's shoes, what comes out is spoken in loving-kindness, even if it is not pleasant to say or hear. It's not so much about seeking and finding agreement with the other as it is creating the space to simply know we have been heard. This allows us to be highly committed to our communication, with a low attachment to winning or losing the issue at hand. I am convinced that we can say just about anything to anybody if it is said with genuine loving-kindness and compassion, with a skillfulness that does not include an agenda to hurt or inflict pain but to simply communicate.

We can learn to be honest in all of our relationships without being brutal. It requires nothing more than conscious intention to make yourself heard in a manner that is nonthreatening, nonshaming, and peaceful. The best place to start this process is with those closest to you. They are the ones with whom we tend to be the most brutal in our communication. Is this is always easy? Of course not! But if we don't start somewhere, we will get nowhere!

Mindfulness Practice

❦ In all of your relationships and communications today, remember that the emotional charge that most often causes people to speak brutally (or harshly) is fueled by the energy of fear. It may be wearing the disguise of anger, frustration, disappointment, impatience, and so on, but it is really only fear in disguise.

❦ Love is the antidote for fear. Remember that God in Its highest form is unconditioned love.

❦ Invite God's presence into your conversations. See the presence of God in the eyes of the person with whom you are communicating and feel that presence at the center of your own being.

❦ Then, let God do the talking. The dialogue will be cushioned in loving-kindness, reverence, and respect. Remember, it's not what you say, it's how you say it.

5

THINGS DON'T
CHANGE, WE DO

*Tomorrow, you promise yourself, will be different,
yet tomorrow is too often a repetition of today.*

~James T. McCay

I have been going to the same bank for seventeen years and have become known by many of the long-time employees there as a good listener. Recently, I had an interesting conversation with one of the tellers that I would like to share with you. I had no sooner extended my normal "howzitgoin?" and she began an instant download and diatribe about her 32-year-old son who she can't get to leave home, saying that "he doesn't work, help with living expenses, or even clean up his room." I just smiled and listened intently to her story until she said something so juicy, so ripe for reply, I could not let it pass. She said, "I can't wait for next year to get here." I asked why. She replied, "Because it has to be better than this year." "Why is that?" I asked. "Just because it is a new year, I guess; maybe things will change," she responded. I told her that the only problem with her theory is that life is much like watching a poorly written and produced play: The next act will be no better than the last one. Likewise, she will have the same son living in the same home in two weeks as she does now—nothing will change but the dates. If thirty years hasn't done it, a week and a half doesn't stand a chance! At that point, I was moved to share one of my favorite sayings with her: "Things don't change, we do. With that in mind, always remember, wherever you go, there you are!"

She laughed and said, "Exactly right . . . now tell me what that means." I told her that it meant if she didn't address the problem now, next year would be a repeat of this one. Beyond that, perhaps the real problem isn't her son but rather how she feels about herself regarding her son. I suggested that she had two choices. Either one of them would work if she could make peace with them. Number one: She could change her mind about her willingness to tolerate the situation even a day longer and muster up the courage and self-acceptance to request that he leave and mean it. Number two: She could choose to change her perception and accept him and the circumstances just as they are and turn it into a nonproblem. Either choice would require a certain degree of acceptance and change on her part, but the result would be some sense of inner peace.

How about you? Is there an issue going on in your life today that you are hoping will just sort of magically change by itself next year? Generally, that's not how to rid yourself of your problems, is it? As Mark Twain said, denial ain't just a river in Egypt. Perhaps, like my teller friend, you need to look clearly at your options. See which one would honor you and those involved in your issue thus bringing you the most authentic experience of inner peace possible. What can you do today to begin to deal with your problem in a proactive manner? What action can you take? It might include asking a trusted friend, mentor, or counselor for some support and honest feedback. It could also include making space available in your mind and heart for God's presence to be more fully revealed, because with your willingness, that presence becomes an incredible guidance system. Isn't it great to know you always have a choice? Make a decision today to either accept what is or do something about it. Stop swimming in the river of denial because it's polluted with hidden resentment (toward yourself as well as others) and fear . . . and because it gets you nowhere fast.

Mindfulness Practice

- Take thirty minutes today to journal. Write down all thoughts that come to you regarding any issues you may have been avoiding (or denying).

- Allow yourself to explore any fears either logical or illogical that could be the invisible strings that support your lack of willingness to deal with the issue.

- Note your feelings. Are you honoring them?

- Then make a commitment to yourself to take a proactive step toward resolving the issue by writing down the date by which you will do it or simply write down these words: As of now, I declare this issue a nonproblem by fully accepting it just the way it is.

- Then take a deep breath and smile. Remember, things don't change, we do.

6 WHAT IS YOUR MESSAGE TO THE WORLD?

My life is my message.

~Mahatma Gandhi

Has there ever been a time in your life when your actions differed from your words and beliefs? If you are like most people (including myself), there are times when it may be hard to walk the talk. It is easy to speak our truth when we are around those who openly support and agree with us. On the other hand, it can be a bit more challenging to stand in our truth, walking the talk, when there are people around us who have different beliefs or opposing points of view. The need for approval can be an interesting trap; if we are not careful, it can woo us into compromising our integrity. When that happens, it usually spills over into many different areas of our life. Then what do we really have left except a life that is lived in the darkened shadows of our own self-doubt and diminished self-respect? Developing consistency between what we believe and demonstrating it by how we live in the world is one of the greatest challenges life has to offer, and it is also the mark of a spiritually evolving individual. Spiritually mature people cannot be bought by the world's opinions.

When I think of lives lived with spiritual integrity, I think of people like Mahatma Gandhi and Martin Luther King. These men walked their talk. Gandhi was a great example of an individual who, by his actions, told the world who he was, what he valued, and what he stood for. Not only did he talk the talk, he walked the talk. His life was a classic example of the old adage "actions speak louder than words." Likewise, Martin Luther King was unbending in his commitment to showing the world who he knew himself to be. I have often wondered what gives people like Gandhi and King the fortitude to stand in their truth and live it . . . to actually be it even in the face of violent opposition. I believe it had everything to do with the relationship they had with their God. It fully enveloped them to the point that they became what they believed. Spirituality, compassion, loving-kindness, integrity, equality, nonjudgment, and nonviolence are words synonymous with both of these great men. Their lives became their message and the world knew it.

You and I are no different. We all have a message to bring to the world. That is why we are here. Ralph Waldo Emerson wrote, "What you are speaks so loudly, I can't hear a word you say." What is your message to the world? For what do you stand? Are you committed to living it 24/7, irrespective of whom you are with or where you may be? What role does your relationship with God play in your message? Once you have this clarity, your life will automatically become your message because you will live authentically from the inside out, allowing the presence of God within to permeate the essence of your every thought, driving every word, deed, and action. How you choose to express what you are makes it your message. Now more than ever, the world needs your message. Gandhi and King knew it. So do you and I. Let's walk the talk together.

Mindfulness Practice

 Become the observer of your words and actions today.

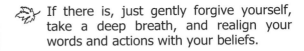 Listen to what you say and witness how you act. Do those things change according to whose company you are in? Do you find yourself compromising what you believe in order to accommodate others? Is there any inconsistency between what you know to be your truth and how you are showing up in the world today?

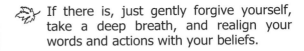 If there is, just gently forgive yourself, take a deep breath, and realign your words and actions with your beliefs.

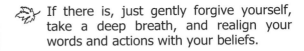 Then, with great mindfulness, walk the talk because what you are does truly speak volumes more than what you say.

7

ELVIS HAS LEFT THE BUILDING

There is a time in every man's education when he arrives at the conviction that envy is ignorance; that imitation is suicide . . .

~Ralph Waldo Emerson

I recently saw an old movie featuring a scene in Las Vegas where an Elvis impersonators convention was being held. There were hundreds of Elvis's (or would that be Elvi?) each doing his personal best to "be" Elvis. There were tall Elvis's and short Elvis's, Black Elvis's and Asian Elvis's, fat Elvis's and skinny Elvis's. The one thing they all had in common was that they were each trying to be someone they were not. While this was a comedy and I took it as such, it still made me think about how often many of us do the same thing in our lives. We go to great extremes to be like someone else, and like the Elvis impersonators, some of us tend to make a career out of it. Wall Street marketers prey on this human need. That is why they pay celebrities millions of dollars for endorsing their products. We buy the product because we want to be like them. It is usually because we admire that person (or perhaps envy them) and while imitation may be the greatest form of flattery (for them), it really isn't honoring the God of our being.

In today's quote, Emerson makes it clear that we were not sent here to try to imitate or duplicate what another person is or has. We are meant to be a unique, one-of-a-kind expression of the divine. God does not need two of anything because that would be redundant and duplicative, neither of which serves in the unfolding, expanding creative nature of the divine. When we try to copy another person, a little part of our unique essence evaporates. That is a form of "emotional suicide," is it not?

One day at a place that made photocopies, I complained to the clerk that my duplicates were splotchy. He replied to me, "These are only copies, sir, they will never be as clear as the original master." Be clear today. Know that you are an original master. You are an original because God has no need for duplicity. You become a master once you begin the daily practice of being yourself. It is hard to be an original in a photocopy world, but the reward is great. You can look into the mirror and say, "Ladies and gentlemen . . . Elvis has left the building!" Honor God today: Be who you came to be.

Mindfulness Practice

- Take time out and find a garden.

- Notice that while all the flowers may at first appear similar, as you look carefully, you will discover each is unique in some way in its marking, color, shape, or size.

- Become aware of the life force that animates the flower, actually expressing its unified self so uniquely.

- Finally, explore the uniqueness of the people around you. If you look deeply enough, you will discover the same thing. You were not meant to be exactly like anyone else.

- Life seeks unique expression through all of its creation, including you. Honor and celebrate it.

8   SEEK SANGHA

*Sangha means spiritual community, and it is
treasured because without it awakening cannot be
sustained.*

~Jack Kornfield

*Building a Sangha, supporting a Sangha, being
with a Sangha, receiving the support and guidance
of a Sangha is a practice . . . when you build a
Sangha that has happiness, joy and peace, you'll see
the element of holiness in the Sangha.*

~Thich Nhat Hahn

She gave me a generous and heartfelt hug as she went through the
reception line exiting our service one Sunday, and with tears in her
eyes, said, "I had no idea that a church could feel so warm, joyous, and
fun . . . and on top of that, I feel so spiritually fed. I feel like I have
known these people for years, and this is my first time. I feel so
comfortable here and I'm not certain why." I replied, "Perhaps it's
because you feel the presence of God making Itself known to you as
unconditional love through the people here." Well, then she really
began to cry, but it wasn't a painful cry, it was a joyful one. There was
a place within her that recognized she was home and she realized it.
The operative word in this conversation is "feel." She had the
opportunity to experience what God's presence felt like, which can be
an overwhelming experience to have in the presence of hundreds of
others.

I believe there is something within each of us that is aching for
authentic spiritual connection, to actually know what God's presence

feels like. Spiritual community is where this happens! Why? Because it creates an environment where everyone feels commonly (communally) and equally embraced in the loving presence of God—it magnifies the experience. Each one actually becomes a reflector for the other, magnifying God's magnificence and love. In truth, spiritual community is necessary for us to be able to fulfill our purpose here on Earth. We need one another to enhance God's experience of loving Itself. It's true that we can and should create this experience alone, in a secluded environment, but ultimately, I believe there can be no greater place for this to happen than in spiritual community. Spiritual masters from all traditions have gone off into the wilderness experience for a period of time to deepen their sense of the sacred, but they know they must return to community to share the truth that they have discovered with others. So, what is it that makes a community a spiritual one? In Eastern teachings, spiritual community is referred to as "Sangha." Sangha is a community of individuals dedicated to creating and sustaining an environment that nurtures and supports reverence, mindfulness, and spirituality as a lifestyle. In Sangha, one of the primary elements created is a feeling of safety. Each one is respected, accepted, and loved as they are—it's a safe place to be who one is. In such an environment, it's amazing to witness each one unfold in their own unique spiritual nature with grace, elegance, and ease in their own time and space. When we add to this the elements of playfulness and Seva (service to others), we have true spiritual community—Sangha. This is a good place to be.

Do you have a spiritual community? Are you sharing sacred space with other like-minded individuals? If not, perhaps now is the time to explore Sangha. You will know when you have connected with the right spiritual community because your heart will make it known to you. Sangha is not a building, it is a consciousness held by a collective group that welcomes, celebrates, and honors you just the way you are. You'll know it, because it's as if you have walked into a wall of love, immersing you in it in the most amazing way! Seek Sangha today.

Mindfulness
Practice

≈≫ If you are already a dedicated member of a spiritual community, make a commitment to invite a friend to accompany you to your next gathering. Extend yourself to others and generously support your Sangha—it benefits all.

≈≫ If you are not a member of a spiritual community, seek one out and be open to the experience. Go with no expectations and an open heart. Don't put it off any longer . . . do it this week!

≈≫ Judge not a spiritual community by its size. Remember: Where two or more are gathered, there too is the presence you seek. Celebrate it!

MAKE TODAY BIG WITH BLESSINGS!

Blessing: Constructive thought directed toward anyone or condition. You bless a man when you recognize the divinity in him.

~Dr. Ernest Holmes

I will forever remember the time our spiritual community hosted a yogi from India as he was touring the country. He was a very sweet, elderly man, looking very much like an Avatar or wise man with the saffron robe, sandals, and long beard. It must have been a sight to behold for our members as he walked through the door of the center. He was a full foot shorter than me (that's pretty short), and the very first thing he did even before we were formally introduced was to reach up and place his hand on the top of my head, saying something in Hindi that I later came to understand was a blessing. Well, that made me feel very special. Ever since that day, I have made a conscious practice of blessing others; however, I seldom put my hand on their head because they might be more startled than I was. With the exception of formal ceremonies, most of the blessing I do for others are done in consciousness, in the silence of my own mind and heart; most often, they don't even know about it. How a blessing is done is not as important as the fact that it is done mindfully. There is nothing magical or mystical about conferring a blessing—it's simply confirming the presence of God at the center of that which is being blessed.

Masters, teachers, sages, and saints from every spiritual tradition have always used blessings as a way to consecrate, sanctify, purify, and heal. Wedding ceremonies, memorial services, christenings, meals, as well as many homes, pets, cars, planes, trains, and everything in between have at one time or another been blessed. The fact is that one need not be a yogi, minister, or spiritual master to confer a blessing. Anyone can offer a blessing because anyone can confirm the presence of God within themselves or others at any event as well as in any condition. The problem is that when things are "good," it often seems easy to forget to bless our lives and the lives of others. Ralph Waldo Emerson wrote, "Never lose an opportunity of seeing anything that is beautiful; for beauty is God's handwriting—a wayside sacrament. Welcome it in every fair face, in every fair sky, in every fair flower, and thank God for it as a cup of blessing." We can bless what's good in our lives, but blessings can become even more meaningful if we remember to bless the bad times as well. Those are the times we need to most remember to remember the truth—God is present then and there as well.

Getting in the habit of daily blessings is a good spiritual practice for us as we evolve. It's actually a matter of remembering that the real blessing has already been bestowed—the gift of life itself. Take a moment to contemplate this and seal it in consciousness by affirming to yourself, "I am blessed and I am a blessing." And, in the process, remember that "I am" is also the name God—you are truly blessed. In the words of Mary Baker Eddy, "To those leaning on the sustaining infinite, today is big with blessings." Now, go forth and bless life as you have been blessed.

Daily Blessings

Mindfulness
Practice

- Remembering that to confer a blessing is simply to confirm the presence of God at the center and circumference of that which you are blessing. Where can you begin blessing life today?

- Perhaps a logical place to start could be by blessing your home and family. Say, "I bless this home, knowing and accepting that God's loving presence enfolds it and every person in it."

- You might want to bless your workplace by saying, "I bless my place of employment and everyone with whom I work, knowing that God's integrity, infinite wisdom, and compassion moves through me and all who enter these doors."

- You could even bless your car before you pull out of your drive way by saying, "This automobile is blessed by the presence of God, which manifests as divine protection and perfect working order. As I enter the flow of life with grace and ease, I am guided effortlessly and safely to my place of destination by God's loving presence."

- Now you have the idea! Bless life today, and you shall be blessed.

10　　LOVE IS ALL YOU NEED

If you want to experience love, you have to start by loving yourself. First you have to love your body, then those who are related to your body, and then the master of the body, the inner Self . . . The truth is that God has no physical body; the only body He has is the body of love. If the love you experience in your daily life — the little love you feel for your friends, your relatives, your pets, and even your possessions — could be turned toward the inner Self, that would be enough to bring you liberation.

~Swami Muktananda

In the early '60s when the Beatles sang "All You Need Is Love," the world sang along as a new generation began searching for love and the meaning of love. While many have found love because they knew the first place to look for it was within, others are still seeking it and continue to look for it in a number of ways. It reminds me of the old country song "Lookin' for Love in All the Wrong Places." We all have an innate drive (and right) to experience love because we are born hardwired with that desire. How so? Spiritually speaking, God is all that is, and in Its highest essence, God is love. This makes you and me divine conduits of God's love. You could say that we were literally born to love, and as corny as it sounds, it does have to begin with loving ourselves first. The old saying "as within, so without" really applies here. We have to discover love within ourselves before we can extend it to the world. Yes, we're talking about authentic self-love here—the love of God. True self-love does not mean ego-centered love (EGO = edging God out) but actually just the opposite. It means getting our little selves out of the way and allowing God to do the loving through us. Self-love is the key that unlocks the door to loving others and our world. As Swami Muktananda states above, an authentic experience of love has to start with fully loving ourselves and all that it encompasses.

This essentially means that any effort to love others without first having the ability to love ourselves will not be authentic. As we become skilled in truly loving ourselves, from the inside out, we can then extend that love to the body of our relationships with others. So, the question has to be, Are we able to love ourselves authentically today? Do we have reverence for our physical bodies as well as for the divine essence that indwells our bodies? Do we respect who we are and what we stand for as human beings as well as spiritual beings? If there is room for improvement in this area, there is no time like the present to begin. Humankind desperately needs to learn how to love itself more completely. Pierre Teilhard de Chardin wrote, "Love alone can unite living beings so as to complete and fulfill them . . . for it alone joins them by what is deepest in themselves. All we need is to imagine our ability to love developing until it embraces the totality of men and of the earth."

The Beatles were on the right track when they sang "All you need is love," because love is all you need . . . but perhaps the title to the song really should have been "All You Are Is Love." That's the truth . . . yeah, yeah, yeah. So, get your little self out of the way and let God do the loving today.

Mindfulness
Practice

🍂 Have you been looking for love in all the wrong places? Following is an exercise to determine your current "love-ability" (ability to love) quotient.

🍂 Go to a mirror right now and look into your own eyes. Do you see a sacred being looking back at you? Keep doing this exercise until you do because it is the key to authentic love.

🍂 Continue to peel away any layers of self-criticism and judgment you may discover until you see only the face of love. What would you do differently if you really saw yourself as a sacred being? How would you treat your body temple differently? How would you treat others differently, knowing that they too are sacred beings?

🍂 You are here to love, so start today! Start with yourself and then work your way out to the world. As within, so without.

11 GREAT EXPECTATIONS!

*Our environment, the world in which we live and
work, is a mirror of our attitudes and expectations.*

~Earl Nightingale

Once upon a time, a traveler from a far and distant town approached a wise man that was just leaving the city into which the traveler was entering. The traveler stopped the wise man and said, "Can you tell me about the city from whence you have just come? What is the quality and character of the citizens here?" The wise man replied, "First stranger, tell me: What were the people like in the last town you visited?" The traveler replied, "Oh, they were a cold bunch of people with no kind words for anyone. It was not a happy town; they were very judgmental and the people were mean spirited and unwelcoming. I couldn't get out of that town fast enough." The wise man paused and then replied, "Ahhh . . . I believe you will discover that the citizens of this town are exactly the same." A short distance further down the road, the wise man encountered another distant traveler entering the city. And likewise, the traveler asked the same question of the wise man, saying, "What is the quality and character of the citizens of this city, sir?" Again, the wise man replied, "First stranger, tell me: What were the people like in the last town you visited?" The traveler replied, "Oh, they were an amazing group of people! They were outgoing and friendly and welcomed me with open arms. They were unconditionally loving and I felt like each one was my brother or sister . . . .Oh, I miss them greatly." The wise man paused and then replied, "Ahhh . . . I believe you will discover that the citizens of this town are exactly the same."

I am uncertain of the origin of this story, but it makes the point very well, doesn't it? Life tends to respond to our outlook. It shapes itself to meet our expectations, which are birthed in our consciousness. In the words of author Jon Kabat-Zinn, "Wherever you go, there you are." In other words, wherever you go on the journey called life, you project your attitude and expectations ahead of you, and life can only be a divine reflector of your consciousness, drawing to you the people, events, and circumstances that reflect what you expect to find when you get there. You might keep this in mind the next time you go to that party or business meeting with people you may feel less than loving toward or the next time you speak with that ex-spouse or the next time you go into any other environment where, up until now, you may have generally expected the worst from people rather than the best. The secret of the ages is to learn to have great expectations with a very low attachment to the outcome. If you can achieve this, you will discover what true inner peace means.

What I have discovered is that what I expect from others is what I get. People generally live up to or down to the level that I expect. Why? Because the energy that I radiate (broadcast) can only draw to me more of the same, that's why. On a very practical level, give some thought to this principle before you take off on a vacation, walk into the post office or the grocery store, and most certainly, before you enter your home. What will you expect your experience to be? Because as any wise man (or woman) knows, you will find the people there to be exactly like you expect them to be. What will you expect of others? Start with yourself: What is the character and quality of the person who lives in your skin? Ahhh . . . as within so without, yes?

Mindfulness Practice

- For the next twenty-four hours, pay particular attention to the altitude of your attitude wherever you go. As you enter a restaurant, pull into a gas station, walk into church, go into the office, and so on, mindfully consider what are you are expecting before you arrive there.

- If you catch yourself expecting less than the best others have to offer, revisit your own intentions and make an adjustment in the altitude of your attitude. Choose to be the one who brings the light with you.

- Realize that you are broadcasting to the universe exactly the experience you expect it to be.

- Remember, the universe always says yes!

12   EXPRESS THYSELF

Everyone has talent. What is rare is the courage to
follow the talent to the dark place where it leads.

~Erica Jong

In my early, lean days as a musician and while attending college, one of the things I did to earn money to pay the rent was to teach music privately. My students ranged from eight to eighty years of age, and the levels of their natural talent were often very high. What I found the most frustrating about teaching was that in many cases, I was able to recognize their talent but they could not (or would not) see it in themselves. After six months of lessons, some of them would throw in the towel. I believe that for at least some of them, their own fear held them back because they knew if their music started sounding too good, then they would have to do something with it! We held recitals every six months, which would flush them out of their "box" or comfort zone. I saw so much awesome talent and potential choked back by fear and uncertainty!

Henry David Thoreau wrote that "most men lead lives of quiet desperation and go to the grave with the song still in them." The song of which Thoreau is speaking is the unexpressed self, God's creative essence looking for an outlet. What I learned from my students and from the pursuit of my own career as a writer and performer was that it requires courage to sing our song. That courage will indeed take us to the very edge of our comfort zone, that dark place called fear: fear of rejection, fear of failure, and perhaps even fear of success. The only thing worse than failing at something is succeeding and not feeling worthy of the success. We will inevitably find some way to undermine that success.) Fear of failure and rejection on the other hand seems to be an issue (attachment) most all of us have the opportunity to heal if we are going to be fully expressed in bringing the gift of who we are to life. It's like "Oh my God, what will I do if they don't like my song?" Get over it! You are singing your song for you not them! Your "song" may not be music at all, but it will be something that gives greater expression to your divine nature, to the divinity of God that flows through you. Sing your song for all your worth!

Mindfulness
Practice

✍ Perhaps your unsung song is dancing, sewing, juggling, gardening, cooking, or _____ (fill in the blank). (It may also be found and expressed through a new dimension in your career.)

✍ Regardless of what it might be, make a commitment to share some talent or creative self-expression you have been holding back from the world with at least three people. It is time to come to the edge of that dark place. ✔

✍ Not to worry . . . God, the ultimate light, is right there with you. So go ahead . . . you've got the spotlight, sing!

13   PLATEAUS, PEAKS, AND VALLEYS

Man can climb to the highest summits, but he cannot dwell there long.

~George Bernard Shaw

Yea though I walk through the valley of the shadow of death, I don't have to stop and build a condo there.

~Tom Costa

I had a conversation with one of my spiritual teachers one day when I told him I had been "stuck in the yuck" on my spiritual path and was feeling very depressed about it. He smiled and said, "I have some good news for you, and I have some bad news for you. The bad news is, life is but a continuum of plateaus, peaks, and valleys that just goes on and on and on until the day you leave the planet. And the good news is, life is but a continuum of plateaus, peaks, and valleys that just goes on and on and on until the day you leave the planet." The point he was making was that irrespective of how I chose to see it, life is a journey, a cycle of ups and downs and in-betweens, and I would never get to the ups without also going through some downs and in-betweens along the way. The challenge for me was that I would have preferred to set up camp at the peak and stayed there. Who wouldn't prefer those high micromoments when time seems to stand still and God's grace is so strongly felt that everything just flows with effortless ease as heaven and earth come together. The simple truth is that peak experiences resonate far greater with most of us than being stuck in the yuck, in the "valley of darkness" where things are often palpably unpleasant, painful, even filled with moments of isolation, despair, fear, and a sense of separation from life and God.

So let's get real. Imagine a heartbeat monitor in the hospital that goes "beep . . . beep . . . beep" with that little blip on the screen that bounces up and down between two extremes. That's a good sign! When it stops beeping and blipping, it's not a good sign—a flatline indicates death. So it is with each of us on our journey through life. We can think of the plateaus in our life as those in-between times that separate the highs and the lows on our journey of spiritual evolution. The ups and the downs in our life require forward movement on our part and can help us maintain our sense of being fully alive. We need the valleys as well as the peaks and plateaus in-between. The key is not to get too comfortable at any of those levels, because our beeps and blips may cease beeping and blipping, which is not a good thing. So, give thanks for having both extremes and the in-betweens as well because it's proof we are alive! Plus, without the low times in our lives, we wouldn't appreciate the highs nearly as much. Contrast is the fiber of our existence that holds it all together.

More than likely, every person reading this has at one time or another been stuck in the valley experience. You may feel like you are stuck in the valley right now, overshadowed by some condition or problem, be it emotional or physical. That's where the good news comes in! You don't have to stay there. There is another peak that lies directly ahead of you. You just need to keep moving through the valley and refuse to take up residence there. The reality is that all of the peaks and valleys we experience happen in our mind. It has little to do with conditions, it's how we perceive them. Don't ever confuse wholeness and a life worth living with a condition. Wholeness is a state of being where we realize we are one with God, irrespective of where we are on the journey. In those times when we feel a bit stuck in the valley, we can remind ourselves that there is as much of God present there as when we are at the peak. The only difference is, at the peak it's a little easier to sense that this is so. If God is all there is, it can be no other way. God is right where we are! It's our awareness of infinite omnipresence in every moment that determines if we are down in the valley or up at the peak. So, I have some good news for you, and I have some bad news for you, and you get to choose which it shall be! Beep . . . beep . . . beep!

Mindfulness Practice	

Mindfulness Practice

↪ Where in your journey are you today? Are you on a plateau, a peak, or in the valley? Take a moment and contemplate this question.

↪ Whichever it is, have you become too comfortable there? Do you feel stuck there?

↪ If you are on the peak, you can take what you know as your truth and carry it down the hill into life and use it.

↪ If you are stuck in the valley, commit to taking some action today to move forward. Call a practitioner, minister, or other trusted friend and ask for support. Give the universe a sign that you are ready to move out of the valley and get ready to break camp!

14   THE RHYTHM OF REALITY

*There seems to be a kind of order in the universe, in
the movement of the stars and the turning of the
earth and the changing of the seasons, and even in
the cycle of human life.*

~Katherine Anne Porter

Early this morning, I took my daily trek down to my meditation
garden, which is located in the middle of a grove of fruit trees,
including pomegranate, orange, avocado, plum, apple, and peach. It
being nearly the middle of November, some of them are beginning to
shed their leaves, which is natural for fall in Southern California. What
took me by surprise were two peach trees standing not more than forty
feet from one another. One tree had lost every leaf on it and appeared
to be preparing for winter's sleep. The other tree, however, still had
every leaf on it and yet had not yielded half the fruit as the one gone
dormant so early! "How can this be?" I thought. Both trees were
planted at the same time and came from the same nursery. How can
they have such different cycles and produce such different yield and
quality of fruit? How can one tree still appear to be so full of life and
the other appear to be void of all life force, given all other facts appear
to be common and equal? I began to wonder if the trees in my orchard
were each subject to their own "tree karma." If we are at all in tune
with the principle of life, the answer is obvious: Every living thing has
its own rhythm, even within the cycle of seasons, that dictates its
expression and experience of life as a species.

As propitious timing would have it, my friend Myrna came to see
me this morning (thankfully, after my walk to the meditation
garden), and she shared with me that she had just lost a dear friend

to pancreatic cancer. Being a spiritually grounded person, she was at peace in knowing that her friend has simply entered through the next door on his journey as an evolving soul. However, what did bother her deeply was the fact that he was still a young man who "had a lot more living to do here on this planet" when he succumbed to this disease. "It just didn't seem fair," she said. I shared with her my observation regarding the two peach trees and as compassionately as possible I said, "Nowhere is it written that life is fair. Life is life and every living thing, including you, me, and your friend, has its own rhythm and season for growth. We come and we go according to the inherent divine intelligence within that knows when it's time to bear our fruit, adding what we have come to add to this earth expression, and when it's time to shed our physical shell and move on to what is next."

Lao-Tzu wrote, "Life is a series of natural and spontaneous changes. Don't resist them—that only creates sorrow. Let reality be reality. Let things flow naturally forward in whatever way they like." My understanding of this statement is that we suffer when we judge that the quality of our life is defined by a long growing season. Let us not mistake quantity with quality. As I learned with my peach trees, the sweetness of the fruit is not necessarily determined by which tree clings to its leaves the longest. Our lesson is to let go and let God . . . and trust the process.

Mindfulness Practice

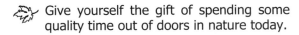 Give yourself the gift of spending some quality time out of doors in nature today.

Observe how the trees that change with the seasons don't struggle to hold on to foliage. They need release in order to be complete in their cycle of growth, preparing for what comes next in their evolution as "tree."

Also notice that not all trees are on the same time schedule. See if you can attune yourself with the rhythm of life to which each tree is responding.

Sense the grace and ease that is present there and invite that energy to move through you.

Know that you and every person you have ever had in your life moves to that divine ebb and flow. Feel the rhythm of your reality and let it have its way.

Notice that the result of doing so is a realization of peace that passes all understanding.

15   LOVE, SERVE, AND REMEMBER

Service is the rent we pay for the privilege of living on this earth. It is the very purpose of life, and not something you do in your spare time.

~Shirley Chisholm

Imagine our world without all the individuals and organizations whose sole purpose it is to serve other people and who do so just for the sake of making a difference in the lives of others and making our country and the world a better place in which to live. In truth, organizations in and of themselves are nothing; it is the individuals who serve others through those organizations who make the difference. Think about this: Without these selfless and caring individuals, there would be no American Red Cross, no hospice organizations, no United Way, no service groups such as Rotarians, Kiwanis, Optimists, Boys & Girls Club, YMCA, YWCA, no Braille Institute, no Salvation Army, no homeless shelters or shelters for abused people, no free clinics, no Habitat For Humanity, no community volunteer groups, and no churches, synagogues, temples, or mosques. As you undoubtedly realize by now, this list could be much longer, couldn't it?

A world devoid of these types of people and service organizations would be beyond devastating. It would be a truly cold and desolate place in which to live. So, the question I ask you to ponder today is, What is it that exists in the hearts of those individuals who serve for the betterment of humanity that inspires them to do so? Surely, qualities such as compassion, loving–kindness, and generosity come to mind, and yet there is more to it than that. I believe most of these people have a deep inner calling, a knowing (whether they are consciously aware of it or not) that they have come to this planet to add their unique energy to the evolving soul of humankind. I believe that we have all come with this calling, it is just a matter of waking up—becoming fully conscious and remembering it. In one of my favorite songs titled "Love, Serve and Remember," John Astin sings, "Why have you come to earth, do you remember? Why have you taken birth? Why have you come? To love, serve and remember . . . to love, serve and remember . . . to love, serve and remember to love."

I ask you now to live in this question: Why have you come to earth and why have you taken birth at this particular time? The answer lies within. As you awaken to the presence of God within you, you will remember and the answer will be revealed. By taking birth, you and I have come here to touch life in a way no other person can, leaving this planet a better place than it was when we arrived. In the East, this is referred to as Seva, which is a Sanskrit word that means "selfless service dedicated to God." Does this mean you have to be part of a service organization in order to love, serve, and remember why you have taken birth? Perhaps so, perhaps not, that is for you to discover. But make no mistake about it, service is not something you do only in your spare time. Every person in your life is there as an opportunity for you to remember why you have come to earth. Every person, every event, every circumstance you encounter offers you a gift: yet another chance to love, serve, and remember to love. That's why you are here.

Mindfulness Practice

➤ If you are not already involved in giving service somewhere in your life, work at getting clear on why that has been so.

➤ Explore these questions: Is it a belief that somebody else will do it? Is it a matter of time and priorities? Is it a lack of motivation? Is it a matter of not knowing where to begin?

➤ Now rethink my opening question: Can you imagine a world without all of the individuals and service organizations whose sole purpose it is to make your world a better place? Is now the time for you to remember why you are here and become one of them?

16

THAT'S MY STORY...
AND IT'S STICKIN'
TO ME!

If an idiot were to tell you the same story every day
for a year, you would end by believing it.

~Horace Mann

Have you ever had an acquaintance tell you the same story about some trauma drama going on in their life every time you were around them? Then one day the actual trauma drama ended, but the story continued to live on, taking on a life of its own day after day, month after month, and yes, year after year until it became a living legend. Eventually, that story turned into their history, becoming their point of identity, their trademark story that defines who they are in the world. After working with many individuals over the years, I have observed that this storytelling ritual usually has a common theme where the storytellers place themselves in the role of the victim. Somehow, somewhere, sometime, someone did something that hurt him or her. Even in the stories where they had the legitimate right to feel like a victim, at a certain point along the way, they made a choice to stay a victim. The retelling and retelling of their story is how they do it. From this mindset, the story keeps them powerless and stuck exactly where they are in their life. On some level, we have to know that this is precisely what they want.

Now, I intentionally presented this scenario in the third person because it's often easier to see it acted out at a distance in other people's lives than in our own. Nonetheless, you and I have each had a story or trauma drama that at some point helped define who we believed ourselves to be. What is the content and theme of your story? Has the victim been liberated from the bondage of the tale yet? Are you continuing to tell it long after the story ended? Is there any part of your daily life in this moment that is drawing its energy from your hi-story, past misfortunes, disappointments, and less than positive life experiences? If we are not fully conscious, it's easy to become mesmerized by our own story. If we tell it often enough, it really does take on a life of its own, and we end up believing it is the truth of who we are. The result is that we then live small, restrictive, powerless, and unrewarding lives.

There is a great country song titled "That's My Story and I'm Stickin' to It." The truth is that when we retell our stories long after the issue itself is dead, the story is actually "stickin' to us." The first step in peeling that story off is to wake up to this holy instant. Think of the precious energy and time you are wasting on keeping the past alive. The truth is that your life is a miracle and a gift from God. To squander even five minutes of it on your story is not honoring the gift that's been given to you. So, write a new story based in who you are today: a spectacular being who is here on planet earth staring in your own production called LIFE!

Mindfulness Practice	
	🍃 Become the conscious observer of your words today. Listen objectively to what your dialogue reveals.
	🍃 If you catch yourself telling a story that only serves to keep you small or in the powerless victim role, stop and take a deep breath.
	🍃 Then, tell a new story, even if it is only a vision of what can be affirmatively different than what was.
	🍃 Focus on the possibilities. That's a story worth telling.

17   COME TO THE EDGE

Come to the edge, he said. They said: We are afraid.
Come to the edge, he said. They came. He pushed
them . . . and they flew.

~Guillaume Apollinaire

I am blessed to live in an area where there is wildlife all around my home. Just across the street and at the edge of a meadow stands a towering eucalyptus tree, perhaps 150 feet high. For many months now I have been watching two large yellowtail hawks build and attend to a nest at the very top of the tree. With the aid of my binoculars, I can see several little chicks in the nest, and daily I monitor their growth. It is said that when the chicks reach a certain size, their mom simply begins to line the nest with thorns and sharp sticks as a gentle way of encouraging the newborns to take to the sky on their own. The obvious message their mom is giving to her little ones is: Don't get too comfortable here. Beyond a certain point, there can be no more growth in the comfort of your nest, and if you want to be a hawk and soar with the wind, you have to take the risk, come to the edge, and push off.

Because we tend to assign our human emotions to the animal kingdom, I have wondered what might be going through the mother's head as she nudges her chicks to the edge of the nest for their first flight. Is she fearful or concerned for the chicks' life? Of course not, because instinct drives her actions. Something within her that knows that there is something within those babies that knows how to fly. She also knows when they're ready to fly. She knows that her job isn't to teach them to fly but rather to simply be what they are: birds. It's the something within the bird that knows how to be a bird that causes it to fly. Of course, that something is divine intelligence, working at the level of "bird." The awareness for me is that the very same divine intelligence that knows how to make these baby chicks soar is working in, through, and as you and I. It knows how to make us soar through life, excelling above and beyond where we are currently nesting so comfortably. The only difference between the baby chicks and ourselves is that we really resist coming to the edge of our comfort zone, don't we?

I can personally testify as to how difficult it can be to move beyond the comfort of our stuck-ness. It is actually rather amazing how we resist those "thorns and sharp sticks" (i.e., pain) that life continues to place in our comfort zone, urging us to come to the edge of all we know as "safe" and to plunge into the unknown that lies beyond. The reality is that beyond a certain point, there can be no growth in the middle of the box we have created called our comfort zone. Perhaps this is the day for you to come to the edge. Do you believe that there is a divine intelligence within you that knows how to sustain you in your next step of growth, the evolution of your own being? If you do, it's time to come to the edge.

Mindfulness
Practice

- Take some time today to explore where the edge of your nest (comfort zone) is.

- A few suggestions might be to enroll in a class you have always wanted (or been afraid) to take; consider that career change you have been avoiding; for Today extend yourself to someone you have been wanting to get to know but have felt afraid to do so; or examine the dissatisfaction you may be feeling in a relationship and make a decision to address it.

- At the least, make a commitment to yourself to "look over the edge" of your comfort zone and take ownership of whatever fears are holding you back from soaring higher in your expression of life.

- If and when fear arises, try to remember the yellowtail hawk in the nest. Trust that place within you that knows how to sustain you when doing what needs to be done in order for you to be what you came here to be.

- Come to the edge!

18   Take the High Road

*Two roads diverged in a wood, and I — I took the
one less traveled by. And that has made all the
difference.*

~Robert Frost

As a minister, one of the greatest rewards of my job is having the
honor of witnessing what happens to people's lives over a period
of years. Each year, I teach an introductory class on spirituality as a
lifestyle, which occurs over a thirty-two week period. It is not unusual
to have as many as sixty students enroll in the class. The first night of
class, I invite them to look around and notice how many people there
are, because in nine months, half of them will not be. It is not that I am
trying to be negative, but rather I am making a point. It requires
dedication to commit thirty-two weeks of their lives (let alone a
lifetime) to entering the spiritual pathway. After the first six weeks, the
class starts to thin out. One of the challenges with teaching
metaphysics is that many people seem to be searching for the "magic
bullet," the quick fix to some part of their lives they want to change. In
nearly two decades of teaching, I have discovered that everyone wants
to alter something in their lives, but very few really are willing to
change!

I liken the spiritual approach to life as a pathway that is very
narrow or, as Robert Frost said, "less traveled." Why? Because it
requires far more than the average person is willing to invest,
requiring much effort as well as a willingness to go where you have
never been before. I believe it is a telltale sign of our society's
addiction to instant gratification. Let's face it, it is much easier to
travel down a five-lane freeway with the masses than it is to venture

off the road and onto a narrow pathway that takes us into the uncharted back roads of our own divine nature—a place seldom visited. At some point, if we are to affect real and permanent change in our lives, it will demand that we do something differently than we have in the past or are doing currently. It requires time and dedication to change our consciousness. Change is difficult because it requires us to step out of our comfort zone and into the unknown. However, the nice thing about taking the high road is that the view is spectacular! You get a chance to see who you really are. Who you really are is a divine manifestation (or expression) of God, questing to know more of Its own divine nature through you and as you. That is a journey of a lifetime. The question of a lifetime is, Which road will you take?

Mindfulness Practice

 Make a conscious effort to be in touch with your tendency for instant gratification today. What are you putting off doing that really needs your attention today? Notice that addiction to instant gratification runs through all areas of your life.

 Now, take an intentional time-out and spend a few minutes directing your focus of attention solely upon the presence of God within you.

 Visualize yourself walking along a pathway that diverges with another. Choosing to follow the path less traveled, notice the wave of inner peace that follows when you put God first. Can you choose to take this path daily? Nod your head and say, "Of course, I can."

It has been said, "The journey of a lifetime begins with the first step." So, step on out there!

19   STANDING GUARD AT THE TEMPLE GATE!

Most of us give ourselves permission to think many things we don't really believe.

~Dr. James Golden

The above quote by my friend James Golden really hit home when I heard him say the words in a retreat he presented at our center titled "Waking from the Dream." The moment he spoke the words, I began to flash back to certain silent conversations I have had with myself over the years about people and events, and essentially, about life. Much to my chagrin, the realization I had was that on more than one of those occasions, my thoughts about others and myself didn't at all reflect what I really believed spiritually. Clearly, James was right, I had indeed given myself permission to think down when I could have been thinking up. How about you? Have you ever caught yourself thinking below the radar screen of your basic spiritual beliefs? Are there ever special occasions when you give yourself permission to think in a manner that you know is not aligned with your true beliefs about life? The reality is that most of us have been there. The good news is, once we are aware that we are aware of our tendency to think down when we know we could be thinking up, we can change it. Too often, our thinking mind contradicts what the deeper self believes and holds to be true, but we have to be conscious enough to see it before we can do anything about it.

In the scriptures, there is a story that clearly illustrates this challenge, which humankind has been dealing with for millennia. A man brings his ill son before the teacher Jesus and asks that the boy be healed. Jesus asks the father, "Do you believe?" The father replies, "Yes, I do believe . . . but help me with my unbelief."

Perhaps we all could use a little help from time to time with our unbelief, because it's in the darkened shadows of our unbelief that we give ourselves permission to think down rather than up.

In his wonderful book *Stillness Speaks*, Eckhart Tolle writes, "When you realize that there is a voice in your head that pretends to be you and never stops speaking, you are awakening out of your unconscious identification with the stream of thinking. When you notice that voice, you realize you are not the voice—the thinker—but the one who is aware of it. Knowing yourself as the awareness behind the voice is freedom." Of course, most of us know that this level of thinking comes from that place within us where the egoic-self reigns supreme until we decide otherwise. The freedom about which Tolle writes comes the moment we become conscious enough to disidentify with the ego, thus enabling us to become the observer of it. When I say we can disidentify with the ego, I don't mean we should deny it or try to exile it, because we need the ego-self in order to survive in the earth world—it's part of who we are. We simply need to be clear enough to know that there is a larger part of who we are who can and should be in the driver's seat, steering our thinking and actions in a manner that correlates more fully with what we really believe. This larger part of us is of course spirit, which always sits serenely, observing how we choose to conduct our lives, waiting very patiently for us to awaken to its presence. When we do awaken to that presence, we automatically begin to think up.

So, we can revoke the permission we have given ourselves to think down rather than up at any time we choose, but it requires conscious intention. It's about waking up and becoming aware of what thoughts are moving through our minds in every holy instant. To this day, I can hear my mother teaching me as a child how to monitor my thinking by saying, "Son, you have to stand guard at the temple gate." I grew to understand that our temple gate is our conscious mind. It's that entry point wherein every thought you have can be stopped and inspected before it is allowed to slip unnoticed into your deeper unconscious mind or out of your mouth and into the world where it could cause great suffering. Be mindful of the thoughts to which you give permission to dwell in your temple and be sure they support what you believe to be true about life and the relationship you are having with the God of your being. If your thoughts don't live "up" to your highest beliefs, evict them! Awareness is an amazing gift, isn't it?

Mindfulness Practice

⫸ Keep a journal for the next seventy-two hours and monitor the thoughts that try and slip past the temple guard that don't support your core values and deepest beliefs.

⫸ Note each time you catch yourself thinking down rather than up and write an affirmation that states a truth that is directly linked to your highest beliefs about yourself and God in that instance.

⫸ If you catch yourself making excuses so you can think down for a "special occasion" (those are the times when judgment, gossip, anger, and so on seem really justified), stop yourself and call out the temple guard. He or she will know just what to do!

20   JUST GIVE IT ALL UP

It is not enough that one surrenders oneself.
Surrender is to give oneself up to the original cause
of one's being. Do not delude yourself by imagining
such a source to be some God outside you. One's
Source is within oneself. Give yourself up to it.
That means that you should seek the Source and
merge in It.

~Ramana Maharshi

After she told me about her problem and how it had dominated and controlled her life for the past seven years, she looked into my eyes, and on the verge of tears, pleadingly said, "I feel so stuck, and I don't even know which way to turn . . . .Can you help me get out of this problem?" I drew a deep breath and said, "I think you should stop the struggle and just give it all up." With that, the floodgate of emotions busted open and tears really began to flow. At that point, along with a box of Kleenex, I offered an explanation of what I meant. I told her that I didn't mean that she should throw in the towel, implying defeat, but rather that she could give it "up" to her higher power within where the wisdom, intelligence, and power of infinite spirit patiently waits to be called on. This kind of "giving up" is not a defeat, it is divine surrender and actually a spiritual victory of sorts because it's about rising above our egoic selves in order to make space for the light of the truth to shine through and show us the way. Ours is to give "up" to the lead of spirit with abandonment and trust. This concept is not new for most individuals who have been on the spiritual path for any length of time. Members of twelve-step recovery groups are no strangers to this idea either. Understanding that God is omnipotence and omniscience as well as omnipresence, we know that while there may be times when we may not have the strength or answers on how to navigate through the darkness, there is something within us that does.

Many people shut down the minute they hear the word surrender. The word can drudge up some sort of pain or fear from a previous experience, which is often based on a concern of losing control or giving their power to another person. Surrender is about giving up control but not to another person or any situation. The spirit within has no need to garner our personal power because it is already all powerful as well as all knowing. With this in mind, rather than praying in utter desperation, "God, show me the way out (of this mess)," we might actually pray, "God, show me the way in (to a deeper communion with source)," trusting that from that deeper place of knowing, we are always gently led to where we need to be. This then is divine surrender. It can be one of the most challenging things for us to do because it requires us to become still enough to listen. We then willingly and mindfully respond to the guidance we receive rather than react to the conditions by which we feel overwhelmed.

Ramana Maharshi suggests that we seek the source and merge with it. The great teacher Jesus was telling us the same thing when he declared, "Seek and you shall find. Knock and the door shall be opened." He knew that the source would avail Itself to anyone who willingly, intentionally, and mindfully merges with It. God has really made this a real no-brainer for us because It is actually seeking us. We don't have to go anywhere to find It because It is constantly knocking on our door. Most of the time, we're just not listening! God is always extending Its guidance, wisdom, strength, and power to us 24/7, but we need to be willing to do our part. Divine surrender is how we do it. Where do we begin? Seek to merge in the infinite flow of life by becoming very still and silently saying, "Show me the way in God, show me the way in." Then, just give it up—let go and literally let God. Trust that the intelligence that breathed the breath of life into you in the first place knows how to get you through even your darkest night of the soul. Just give it all up. Ahhh, sweet surrender!

Mindfulness Practice

✍ Dedicate time today to practice divine surrender, even if you don't feel you have a need for it. You might be surprised after the fact, you may well have had more need of it than you thought.

✍ If you do have a special concern on your mind at this time, while sitting in a quiet and comfortable place, gently hold that concern in a conscious state of awareness and draw in a series of slow, deep cleansing breaths. With each out-breath, imagine you are literally giving it "up" to God. Feel the wave of release that gently moves through you.

✍ With each out-breath, you can even add a series of affirmations, saying something such as "I am open, ready and willing . . . .Show me the way in God . . . .I let go, and I let God . . . .I just give it up right now."

✍ Then, take time to be very still, commune with the source, and listen, knowing that your deepest intentions are always honored.

21

PIERCING THE
VEIL OF EVIL

*There can be no existence of evil as a force to the
healthy-minded individual.*

~William James

Throughout recorded history, there have always been people who
have done evil and horrendous things to others. Senseless acts of
violence, cruelty, and mayhem have been perpetuated from one
millennium to the next; most often targeted are good, innocent, and
usually defenseless people. The terrorist attacks on September 11,
2001, make this point very clear. Not only do we see the same thing
happening daily around the world, but we see it in our own
communities as well. When it happens in our own backyard, the reality
of it cuts even more deeply. It seems more real. With great pain in our
hearts and confusion in our minds, we all search for answers. Why?
How could this happen?

There are many who rush to blame these senseless acts of violence
on history's greatest scapegoat, "the devil," believing (fearing) that
there is some evil power at work. Evil is not a power, it is an action.
While I am the first to agree that there are many people in the world
doing evil things, I do not believe there is an evil power, a prince of
darkness, or any other evil entity. This would mean a duality exists
at the level of spirit (two powers opposing each other) and that's an
absolute impossibility. If there were duality, the entire universe
would be in conflict, and it is not. Only humankind intentionally
harms one another. There is no evil power, only people who misuse
the power they possess in evil ways. So, what is the spiritual
resolution for this problem called evil? The great author Eric
Butterworth writes, "Evil, and evil spirits, devils and devil

possession, are the outgrowth of man's inadequate consciousness of God. We must avoid thinking of evil as a thing in itself—a force that works against man." I am impressed by Dr. Butterworth's description of evil as "an *inadequate* [emphasis added] consciousness of God." How, then, would holding an adequate consciousness of God dispel evil? To hold an adequate consciousness of God means we are living in a moment-to-moment conscious awareness of God's presence, knowing there is but one power operating in us, through us, and as us. In this consciousness, there is no room for the darkness of duality thinking.

It's interesting to note that the word "evil" is "live" spelled backward. Evil finds its point of origin in the mind of a person who is unable to live in the light of God's presence. Evil is born in the mind of one whose vision of life is blurred through the lens of darkness, self-loathing, and hatred, which is then projected onto the world stage and acted upon. Evil is also fear of inferiority, which manifests as feelings and actions of superiority. And finally, evil breeds in the dark corners of a mind that fears it is separate, alone, and apart from life and light. On the other hand, a healthy-minded individual is one whose focus is just the opposite. He or she knows there is a shared connectedness and unity with all life and all people. Life is viewed clearly through the crystalline lens of love, knowing the point of origin for his or her light is at the center of one's own being, where God is found residing.

Then this light is extended to the world, knowing that in the presence of that light, darkness has no power and no reality. He or she lives in the presence of God.

Mindfulness Practice

🍃 Remember, evil is not a power unto itself; evil is an action driven by fear and spiritual ignorance. Don't try to deny that evil exists because doing so just gives more power to the illusion.

🍃 Likewise, as the great teacher Jesus advised us, "Resist not evil." Don't try to combat the appearance of evil, just shine the light on it. How? Make a decision to live life today from the inside out by holding the consciousness of God. As within, so without.

🍃 Make no mistake about it, the light that radiates from within you makes a difference in a world where there appears to be much darkness.

22 SEEK BALANCE IN ALL THINGS

Just as your car runs more smoothly and requires less energy to go faster and farther when the wheels are in perfect alignment, you perform better when your thoughts, feelings, emotions, goals, and values are in balance.

~Brian Tracy

As Buddha sat under the Bodhi Tree waiting for enlightenment, two musicians were arguing about the sound they were trying to get from their stringed instrument and distracted him. He was weak and tired from not eating or taking care of his body, but he wanted to see what was causing the commotion, and so he dragged himself closer to hear them. One musician would tighten the strings and the other would cry, "Not too tight because you will break the string." The other would counter by saying, "Not too loose because the string will only buzz and rattle—in the middle is just right." The master heard the wisdom contained in their argument and declared, "That's it! That's the key . . . perfect balance!" Not too tight yet not too loose, not too high yet not too low, not too in yet not too out. The middle path is the way! Of course, an entire teaching has evolved from this idea of a middle pathway, one that has affected millions of lives in a very positive way.

Excessiveness in any area can prove to be unproductive if not damaging. The Buddha himself had ignored the well-being of his body while trying to free his mind. It caused him to be extremely out of balance. Have you ever had a tendency to be excessive in some area of your life that led to imbalance in other areas? The truth is that all of life is simply energy flowing in certain directions, which we determine by means of our intentions and priorities. If we spread that energy out, allowing it to flow in too many directions, we become cause to our own effect of an imbalanced life. As a result, wholeness and a life worth living are missing in our experience. Many people direct their energy so excessively in one way, ignoring the many other aspects of their lives, that it ultimately catches up with them, making them emotionally drained or possibly ill and most certainly no fun to be around. This is a universal principle with which we can all relate: Some people devote so much time to their work and making lots of money that they forget what it means to play, relax, and spend time with loved ones. Others play so much that they don't know what it is to work. Some people have total disregard for their body temple when it comes to diet and exercise, while others are so obsessed with their diets and bodies that they don't know what it is to take a break and enjoy a day without beating themselves up physically or emotionally. And finally, there are those who are so fanatical about their religious beliefs they don't do anything else but preach and pray, while others could use a bit more preaching and praying.

Do you see yourself in any part of this description of imbalance? If so, perhaps the middle way is a path you may want to explore. Perfect balance: It means not too much, not too little . . . in the middle is just right. Living a balanced life will produce a life of wholeness and deep inner peace.

Mindfulness Practice

Consider these six areas of your life as strings on an instrument: spirituality, physical health, emotional health, relationships, prosperity and job satisfaction, and free time and self-expression.

Invest some time today in exploring which of these strings are in need of tightening and which may need loosening. Make a commitment to fine–tuning your instrument beginning today.

Seek the middle way and notice that your life is fit as a fiddle and in perfect harmony with the universe.

23 THE FORCE IS WITH YOU

*What is needed, rather than running away or
controlling or suppressing or any other resistance,
is understanding fear; that means, watch it, learn
about it, come directly into contact with it. We are
to learn about fear, not how to escape from it.*

~Jiddu Krishnamurti

Do you remember the Star Wars movies? I thought you might be able to relate with a saying that became popular after the first movie came out. It continued to be a predominate theme in all the sequels and was one of the greatest lines used throughout all the Star Wars movies. It was spoken anytime there was a problem brewing: "There is a disturbance in the Force." The "Force" of course is a metaphor for the universe and the law by which it operates. The disturbance was came from the dark side of the Force, where the evil Darth Vader ruled through intimidation and fear. The importance of the message is that there are not two powers, only two ways to use the one power. The storylines in all these movies pitted an ongoing battle between the light side and the dark side of the Force . . . the classic struggle between good and evil, duality. As a metaphysician, I always delight in watching these movies because they depict so perfectly the impartiality of the force, or the law of the universe, and how it can be used to one's advantage or disadvantage, according to his understanding of it and relationship with it.

What I liked best about the master Jedi knight of the light side, Obi Wan, was that he knew that the only power Darth Vader really had was the ability to instill fear in others. That power thus allowed him to use the "force" of their own being against them and to his advantage. Luke Skywalker discovered that as he faced his own fear, studied it, and finally understood it, he was able to defeat the appearance of evil manifested as Darth Vader. Oddly enough, it turns out that his very own father was the lord of the dark side. How often are we the father of our own fear thoughts?

There is much fear in many people's minds today. To some degree, it has immobilized many of us. Perhaps it is time for you and I to turn and face our fears. You have to go no further than the mirror. Fear is an emotion that wells up from within. It does not come from outside of you. It can be stimulated by outside factors, as depicted by the evil Darth Vader, but the fear itself is nothing more (or less) than a feeling that comes from the dark side of your own being when you slip into a belief in duality, losing touch with who you really are. You and I will always have our own personal Darth Vaders to deal with because it is part of the odyssey called life. So, be open and teachable like Luke Skywalker. As you let your fears become your teacher, you will discover that there is nothing wrong with the shadow self because it is part of your human reality. In that process, you will also discover that you are more than a human being . . . you are more than a personality . . . you are more than a body . . . you are more than a shadow. You are the very nature of divine essence, which is pure light. So, the next time you feel a "disturbance in the force" and fear begins to wrap itself around you, don't run from it but embrace it, dance with it, and demand that the light be shed on it. How? Remember, light dispels darkness. Have faith. Step out of your own shadow and into the light of God's presence. In other words, let go of any notions that you are any less than one in God. Fear knocked at the door. Faith answered. No one was there.

Mindfulness
Practice

> ➣ Realize that most of your fears are of the unseen and are attached to the future.

> ➣ While breathing deeply now, make a connection with the greater unseen, God. Feel that presence within and all around you.

> ➣ Now, invite that presence to be the light you carry into this day and know that the force really is with you!

24   GOING TO THE MOUNTAIN TOP

I do benefits for all religions — I'd hate to blow the hereafter on a technicality.

~Bob Hope

While in college, I had a roommate who devoutly went to church each week. The interesting thing was each week he would attend a church of a different denomination "just in case one of them was right," he would say. He considered himself to be a practicing Jew-Catholic-Baptist-Buddhist-Mormon-Methodist. How he managed that I still don't know, but he did. He was serious too. He was so invested in making sure he made it into the hereafter that, at times, I think he forgot what he was "here after." Well, at least I can say my roommate was open-minded.

Once in a while, I will encounter an individual who tells me that while my intentions are good, his or her religion is the only right one. I have discovered that people usually want to debate (argue) religion because they believe that if they win the debate, they must be right. Being right seems to be very important to these individuals because if they are wrong, then what? They may have to go religion shopping, taking them way out of their comfort zone! This kind of fanaticism has always felt fear driven to me. Over the years, I reached a point in my spiritual growth where I no longer needed to debate or defend what I believe to others. I simply smile and thank them for sharing their perspective. My desire is to honor every person's spiritual path even if it differs from mine. I can't do that if I am attached to winning a debate.

If you can, imagine God as a mountain, and at the top lies the full experience of union with the infinite. Now imagine many villages surrounding the mountain at its base, each with its own unique pathway to the top of the mountain. Think of each village as a different religion. Is one pathway better than another path if they all take the devoted follower to the top? In a world with billions of people and thousands of religions, it is spiritual arrogance to say there is only one correct path. The fact is religions are like automobiles, it doesn't matter what kind you drive if it gets you to your destination, which is a one-to-one relationship with God. The key is to drive it daily. So, put the pedal to the metal!

Mindfulness Practice

- As you drive around town passing different churches and various places of worship, bless each one and celebrate them in their ability to transport people to the "top of the mountain."

- Know that each person who attends and supports that church, temple, or mosque is exactly where he or she needs to be on their spiritual pathway.

- Also, celebrate your own chosen pathway and give thanks for all that it provides for you on your journey up the mountain. See you at the top!

25   IT'S ALL A MATTER OF PRIORITIES

*What comes first, the compass or the clock? Before
one can truly manage time (the clock), it is
important to know where you are going, what your
priorities and goals are, in which direction you are
headed (the compass). Where you are headed is more
important than how fast you are going. Rather than
always focusing on what's urgent, learn to focus on
what is really important.*

~Source Unknown

The above quote is a profound and powerful one, isn't it? If you are
like me, too often you put the clock in front of the compass. It is
amazingly easy to get so sucked into what we perceive as the urgency of
the moment, putting out the fires of our daily affairs, that we lose track
of where we have intended our lives to go. As Deepak Chopra would
say, we have forgotten to pay attention to our intention. This is why
taking time to examine our priorities should be a priority. So, my
question for you today is: Is your life moving toward the vision or
intention you have set for yourself or have you become enmeshed in the
minutia of the moment and been pulled off course? This is not a
terribly difficult question to answer. Just check in with your heart and
you will know instantly—in a heartbeat.

I know that the moment at hand with all of its trauma dramas can
seem quite urgent, but in the majority of cases, it is only so because
we have created an importance in our mind that makes it so. This
seems to be a major issue with many of us who are busy building or
sustaining vital careers. Perhaps that comes from an overinflated ego
that has us convinced that we are irreplaceable or that no one else
could manage the problem at hand as well as we can. It may be time

for a reality check, so here is a simple test you can use to determine if the issue currently at hand is truly a priority: give it the 10-year test. Ask yourself, Ten years from now, will what's going on in this moment really matter to me? You will discover that a large majority of the time, the answer will be "no." With this clarity comes a renewal of the awareness of what's truly important. For most of us, when our priorities are clearly seen, what is most important is our relationships. First perhaps, what is the quality of the relationship we are choosing to have with God? This requires great dedication, doesn't it? Then, how about the quality of the relationships we are having with family and friends? It's amazing how we tend to push what is really most important aside when our priorities are not crystal clear.

At the end of your journey on this planet, where will your compass have led you? Today could be the perfect day to take a reading of that compass, and if needed, to set a new course. Take time out, and if appropriate, reprioritize. If you don't, you may not have anyone on your journey with you as you arrive at your final destination . . . and none of us were meant to travel this incredible pathway called life alone.

Mindfulness
Practice

- Take time right now to "freeze frame" your life. Take a very objective and hard look.

- Ask yourself if your current priorities are in alignment with the vision and intention you have set for your life. Does what you are thinking, saying, and doing match that vision?

- If so, congratulations and keep it up!

- If not, get out a pen and paper and make a list of action steps you can initiate today to make it so. Put your priorities in an order that honors and serves you and those you love.

- Then, do the work, remembering that where you are ultimately headed is far more important than the time it will take to get there.

26   RESOLVE TO EVOLVE

*We have come to realize not only what ancient
wisdom has revealed but also what modern science
is now confirming. No one's life is created or
sustained totally by matter or by the body. Bodies
are forms life takes, but bodies don't create life.
Your body isn't creating your life or enlivening
your body. Your life essence swims as an individual
creation in the universal life essence. If there's only
one life, a universal infinite life, then you're an
activity of it. You're a dream that the universal life
is having.*

~Roger Teel, D.D.

*Scientists are in the strange position of being
confronted daily by the indisputable fact of their
own consciousness, yet with no way of explaining
it.*

~Christian de Quincey, Ph.D.

Having just returned from the 2003 Association for Global New
Thought (AGNT) conference in Palm Springs, my head is still
spinning with delight and wonder. I spent a full week emerged in the
very intense collective consciousness of more than two thousand
like-minded individuals, all of whom exuded with absolute certainty

an awareness of their evolving relationship with the universe and interconnectedness with one another. What intensified the entire experience was that along with the AGNT, the Institute of Noetic Sciences (IONS) was the co-presenter for the event. IONS was founded in 1973 by astronaut Edgar Mitchell shortly after his return from his stroll on the moon and is largely made up of individuals from the scientific community. I love the quotes stated above by theologian Roger Teel and scientist Christian de Quincey (both of whom were at the conference) because they illustrate the amazing merging of spirituality and science, which was palpable at the conference. What we learned is that many scientists delight in exploring the unexplainable phenomenon of life expanding upon itself, and their interest is quite often peaked by an awareness that there is some organized intelligence at work that appears to be greater than they. For some scientists, this awareness may well invoke the question, "Am I the observer . . . or am I the observed?" Similarly, while theologians may be less consumed with the mechanics of it all, they want to experience an ever-deepening relationship with that same intelligence, accepting with absolute faith and certainty that they are already one with that which they seek to know more personally. In either case, Dr. Ernest Holmes summarized it beautifully when he wrote, "What you are looking for, you are looking with." This is the awareness that stimulates conscious evolution.

While individuals from each group may or may not have been predisposed to calling this intelligence by name (God, spirit, essence, or presence), what was most amazing was the manner in which all came to a similar conclusion: The universe in which we all exist is a living, intelligent thing. It is animated by some life force that is evolving in substance and form as it expands, constantly pushing out and seeking fuller expression of its own nature through a law of cause and effect. Therefore, every human being is part of the whole and plays a vital role in determining the manner in which we evolve as individuals, and perhaps more important, as a species because we are constantly causing our own collective effect.

The reality is that the universe shall continue to evolve eternally regardless of what we do. The question is, Will we as a species and as passengers on Spaceship Earth evolve along with it? If we don't, we won't be here all that much longer. We know the universal imperative is "grow or die," which is where the conscious evolution of the species kicks in. It also marks the point at which we can begin to collectively learn how to live with reverence for our mother earth, Gaia, as well as our entire earth family. How can we not live with reverence for all of life once we are conscious that we are each interconnected with our mother earth, brother moon, sister star . . . and one another? Our awakening to this truth is the beginning of our conscious evolution. We are on the verge of creating a new paradigm for humanity and as Barbara Marx Hubbard stated at the conference, "We are nearing critical mass and there is a mighty change coming." So, perhaps now really is the time to be still and know: What you are looking for, you are looking with. Can you feel it stirring? I can.

Mindfulness Practice

 What does "be still and know" mean to you? Ponder this question for a few moments. Be in awe of the fact that you can even contemplate your own existence.

 Practice stillness today and see if you can penetrate the layers of your being until you realize that the spiritual experience you are seeking is actually seeking you.

 Now breathe and know you are evolving consciously.

27

For a long time it seemed to me that real life was
about to begin, but there was always some obstacle
in the way. Something had to be got through first,
some unfinished business; time still to be served, a
debt to be paid. Then life would begin. At last it
dawned on me that these obstacles were my life.

~Bette Howland

Webster's dictionary defines an obstacle as "an obstruction that prevents a forward movement or course of action." Do you ever feel restricted by an obstacle—something that keeps you from moving forward with your life, something that stands between you and what you define as a complete and whole life? Do you see the pathway of your life leading to a point at which you will one day arrive where all obstacles will disappear? If you do, you are in for one long pathway. I don't know of anyone who doesn't have obstacles of one kind or another in their life. As a matter of fact, my observation is that often those who appear to have the greatest challenges in life, with apparent obstacles far larger than my own, seem to see their own challenges not as obstacles at all but rather growth opportunities for forward movement. Thomas Carlyle wrote, "The block of granite, which is an obstacle in the pathway of the weak, becomes a stepping-stone in the pathway of the strong." In other words, obstacles are all a matter of perspective. Do you see the challenges in your life as obstacles or opportunities? Do you see them through the eyes of a victim or a victor? Either way, let's free ourselves from any illusions: We shall always have challenges. How we see them is our choice.

I first met Joe LaSalle at our center when he was in his early twenties. Joe uses a wheelchair. He lost the use of both legs when he was a pre-teen, due to leg surgeries gone wrong. For years, it wasn't unusual to see Joe wheeling around town. He even entered special events and competition for those with similar "handicaps." In truth, Joe has never seen himself as handicapped. He became known around town as the Wheelin' Wonder because of his skills on the dance floor and as a musician. He makes that wheelchair do things Elvis would envy. He later became a professional personal fitness trainer and now works with people throughout the city, helping to shape not only their bodies but also their attitudes. How does he get around today? He earned the money to buy a truck, which he had fitted with special equipment that allows him to control the foot pedals with his hands. It would have been very easy for Joe to perceive his circumstances as huge obstacles. Instead, he moved into adulthood with a healthy attitude about his future. He made a decision to see opportunities not obstacles. As a result of his choices, he has become a beacon of inspiration and encouragement for countless others. One of the greatest gifts Joe offers the world is visual proof that wholeness is not a physical condition; it is a state of being. The next time you feel overwhelmed by the obstacles that lie between you and a happy and whole life, I invite you to think of Joe LaSalle.

In Zen, there is an old saying: The obstacle is the path. Know that a whole and happy life is not free of obstacles. Quite the contrary, a whole and happy life is riddled with obstacles—they simply become the very stepping–stones that help lift us to a new perspective. It is not what happens to us in this life that shapes us, it is how we choose to respond to what happens to us. Victim or victor, the choice is ours. As long as we inhabit these garments of flesh and bone, it is a choice we will have the opportunity to make many times over. It is all part of our journey along this wonderful pathway of becoming more of that which we have come to be. Obstacles or opportunities—what say you?

Mindfulness Practice

➤ Are there any obstacles that, until now, have been impeding your forward movement toward a life of wholeness and happiness? If so, understand that it is possible to make a choice to reframe the obstacles and see the opportunities for growth and freedom that lie inherent in them.

➤ The first step may be to invite the divine intelligence within to reveal any need to remain a victim of your circumstance. Victims tend to remain powerless.

➤ It's time to claim your power. Know that your wholeness is not defined by circumstances or external conditions, nor do they determine your future happiness.

➤ Make a choice to see the possibilities for good that can come from those obstacles once you stop seeing them as encumbrances. Notice the power that arises from within that effortlessly transforms those obstacles into opportunities.

➤ The power of perspective is pretty amazing, isn't it? So are you.

28

The unexamined life is not worth living.

~Socrates

One of the greatest blessings (and curses) of walking a spiritual pathway is the ongoing opportunity life presents to us to examine who we are and for what we stand. To live with spiritual integrity means to live our lives from the inside out, turning within and seeing the correlation between our sense of the sacred and the manifestation of it in our daily affairs. The idea of examining our lives on a regular basis is not very appealing to many individuals, to a large degree because they don't like what they see when they take a look. I believe this is why our culture has such an addiction problem with drugs, alcohol, food, and sex. It is much easier to find some method of staying in the dark corner of denial than to step into the light and expose that part of ourselves to life (and the light). It takes courage to turn and face our demons, but it is the only way to true liberation. Notice I didn't say "fight them" . . . just reveal them to the light. The light, of course, is God's presence. After all, what happens to any form of darkness the moment it is exposed to the light? As Emerson said, "It fades away into the nothingness from which it came."

Does this mean our problem automatically vanishes? Perhaps so, perhaps not, but it does mean we will see it from a new perspective, which can be very empowering. Our boogeymen don't seem nearly as scary during the day, do they? The trick is to have the courage and willingness to find the light switch and turn it on. In the book *Love and Law*, Dr. Ernest Holmes writes, "The science of self-mastery is the science of being equal to everything that confronts you. There is nothing too great; there is nothing too big; there is no obstruction you cannot surmount if your concept of the truth is dynamic enough. The truth with which you deal is absolute in every respect, always. All of God, all of truth, all there is, is right there . . .[awaiting] . . . your recognition."

Realize that you and I are here to thrive and excel in our livingness not simply to survive or endure. If you are not thriving and excelling, if at times you feel like your life is just about enduring and surviving one more day, perhaps some self-examination is in order. It all begins with recognition not just of your problem but of a presence bigger than your problem. Start from the inside and work your way to the outer. Find your divine light switch and recognize that at the core of your being is the allness of God. Let that light shine on the dark corners of your mind and see what is revealed. If you look with open eyes, you will like who and what you see.

Mindfulness Practice

➢ Put time aside to begin an honest self-inventory. If you discover there is some aspect of your self or your life with which you are not truly at peace, call it forward in your awareness.

➢ In your mind's eye, place it on an alter. See it as a sacrifice if you choose.

➢ Then call forward an awareness of God's presence as pure white light. Watch as the light simply assimilates the problem, removing it from your life as an obstacle.

➢ Make a habit of facing your demons. You will discover that they have no reality in the light of God's presence.

➢ It is time to stop telling God how big your problem is . . . and start telling your problem how big your God is. Just turn on the light!

29   HOW MUCH IS ENOUGH? PART ONE

Prosperity is not just having things. It is the consciousness that attracts the things. Prosperity is a way of living and thinking, and not just having money or things. Poverty is a way of living and thinking, and not just a lack of money or things.

~Eric Butterworth

When I first entered the consciousness movement in the late 1970s, I think I was still struggling to understand what consciousness was really all about. The one topic that would get more people to attend a class than any other was prosperity. The "me" generation was in high gear and the question "How much is enough?" was the soup de jour. A lot of people were convinced that prosperity was about money and stuff. The logic was this: The more stuff you had the less miserable and more happy you would be. So, many people focused on how to get more. While they may have succeeded in increasing their possessions and net worth, do they now possess more happiness? In most cases, the answer is probably "no"; the only thing that has changed is the nature of their problems. There is no doubt, however, that given the choice, most people would much rather be rich and miserable than poverty stricken and miserable. My question is, Why be miserable at all? As we explore the deeper meaning of prosperity, the answer will become self-evident.

Prosperity isn't about how much stuff you have, it's about a state of consciousness, and likewise, so is poverty. We know another term for consciousness is belief system. A belief system based in "there is not enough" will do one of two things: It will drive people to achieve and get more and more stuff, thinking that the stuff will fill the not-enough hole (rest assured it never will), or it will cause some people to go even deeper into the hopelessness and despair of poverty. They have a demonstration of "not enough" right before their eyes, so it must be true! Their experience simply reinforces the consciousness of lack, and the roots of despair grow even more deeply into the fertile soil of a poverty-minded consciousness. The endless cycle goes on and on and on. In both cases, they are dealing with an effect, while they could be dealing with the cause—their consciousness. Perhaps a new understanding of prosperity might be in order.

I like Dr. Raymond Charles Barker's definition of prosperity. He writes, "Prosperity is having the ability to do what you want to do, when you want to do it." He doesn't mention money or possessions. It's about developing a consciousness that gives one a sense of freedom. Think about it: In truth, that to which we are too attached actually causes us to be in bondage to it. We are not free. With a lack of freedom comes a lack of inner peace and an abundance of discontentment. Does this mean we can't or shouldn't have the wonderful accoutrements and possessions that hard work and good fortune bring? Of course not. The only question is, Do your possessions possess you? Where do we begin to build a consciousness that will bring a prosperity in which we are truly free? Tune in to the next message for part two!

Mindfulness Practice

- Begin to explore what you believe about prosperity.

- Don't focus on your thoughts, focus on the feelings that arise as you challenge what you believe. Is there a feeling of fear or freedom?

- Today, just live in this awareness by asking yourself, How free am I in my everyday life, really? Then experience how you feel.

30   THE DIVINE PARADOX: PART TWO

If you want greater prosperity in your life, start forming a vacuum to receive it.

~Catherine Ponder

One of the greatest paradoxes in life is to be found in the principle of abundance and the law of circulation. Great metaphysicians throughout the ages understood it and taught it to those who would hear. The teacher Jesus imparted this wisdom when he said, "By your standard of measure it shall be measured to you; and more shall be given besides. For whoever has, to him shall more be given; and whoever does not have, even what he has shall be taken away from him." If we were to put it in contemporary language and metaphor, we might phrase it like this: It is done unto you exactly according to your belief. Therefore, if you believe in "more than enough," you will receive even more, and if you believe in "not enough," the universe will conspire to take what little you may have from you. It sounds a bit unfair, but that is how the law of circulation works. Ernest Holmes summarized it beautifully when he stated, "There are no voids because the universe abhors a vacuum." The universe will automatically fill that void according to our beliefs.

Herein lies the paradox: If you want more of whatever it is you desire, you have to first prove to the universe that you are capable of having it by developing a consciousness that affirms there is no shortage of it. The only way to do this is by creating a vacuum or space for it to be received, and the only way you can create a space for it to be received is by letting go of what you do have, trusting that the universe knows what it is doing. That's the law of circulation in action. To people enmeshed in fear of "not enough," this logic will make no sense at all. So they cling and hoard, which simply broadcasts a message to the universe that they lack, to which it responds, "Let me help you prove it." To a person who is established in a conscious awareness of his unity with the source of all good, it can be no clearer. Letting go is a prerequisite for receiving. We can do this more easily when we trust the principle of abundance and the law of circulation.

We now understand that prosperity is more than money; it is what brings us freedom in all areas of life. After you have discovered where you desire more freedom in your life, you will automatically know where you need to begin creating a vacuum to receive. This only happens by first letting go. What does that look like for you? Of what do you need to let go and how do you begin doing that? Tune in to the next message for part three!

Mindfulness Practice

⚜ Imagine your mind as a large storage warehouse that is filled to capacity. There is absolutely no room for anything good to be added. Obviously, something needs to be removed to make room. What might that be?

⚜ Begin to search for the boxes and crates with labels such as fear, not good enough, victim, resentment, the past, the future, lack, and unlovable.

⚜ As you discover them, visualize yourself removing them from the warehouse. See a huge rubbish truck come by, taking it all and hauling it to the dump.

⚜ Now, look at the new space you have created in your warehouse. What will you tell the universe to put there? Hint: Start with "I am enough" and go from there.

31

*Through giving generously, you are entitled to
expect that Life will fill your desires. You alone can
create that expectancy by your willingness to
release the good you hold, in order to receive a
greater good. Once you establish the security of
giving, you will never hesitate to give to a worthy
cause. The beggar who seeks a handout from you
will represent his own consciousness of poverty and
lack; but for you he affords the opportunity to
emphasize your faith in abundance. So you give to
him from your sense of security in life.*

~Dr. Arthur G. Thomas

As the young woman rummaged through her purse trying to find her wallet, she could smell the liquor on the breath of the disheveled old man, waiting patiently for a handout for his "breakfast." As he walked away with a crisp ten–dollar bill clutched tightly in hand, her friend begrudgingly said, "Don't you know you just wasted your money? He will be at the liquor store within five minutes 'drinking' his breakfast." The young woman replied, "Perhaps so, but I didn't give him the money with conditions attached, and I didn't give it to him just for his sake but for my own as well." Her friend looked bewildered and confused by her statement and simply shook her head. The young woman then silently gave thanks for the ability to share her abundance, took a deep appreciative breath, smiled, and continued her walk down the street.

If you could imagine yourself as one of the characters in this story, which one would it be? The young woman clearly understood the law of circulation and the true meaning of abundance. She knew she wasn't giving to get anything; it was how she affirmed her ability to participate in divine circulation and confirm her security in life. Her friend had no clue and the old man didn't care. This is a story about your ability to develop a true prosperity consciousness when you are prepared to enter into the flow of giving. The moral is simple: Give selflessly and with no agenda or strings attached. When appropriate, give mindfully, with compassion and nonjudgment, but most important, give freely. This is the key to creating a life of wholeness. We know we must make room in our lives in order to receive. It is simply how the universe works and it never compromises on this point. The universe is waiting for a sign from you. Whatever you desire more of, you need to start giving. Don't give in order to get but give with the right intention; it is how you confirm you are alive and plugged into life! Money is a great place to start because it is so tangible, and for most people, money has so much fear of "not enough" all around it. Want to see how much fear you may have around money? Consider tithing (tithe means 10% of your financial good) back to the source of where you feel you are being spiritually fed for thirty days as recognition of how abundant your life is.

Dr. Raymond Charles Barker said, "Be clear and free in your money: Be clear that God is the source of all your good and be free to allow it to flow through you." Now, we know that money is simply energy in a specific form. Energy is a universal principle and you are simply a conduit through which it flows. Giving primes the pump for a greater flow, so give the energy of your self to others: Give time, give smiles, give hugs, give service, give rides, give patience, give respect, give forgiveness, give love . . . and most important, give thanks to God for it all.

Mindfulness
Practice

➤ Make a commitment to yourself that within the next twenty-four hours, you will find a way to give that which is meaningful and significant to you.

➤ If you want a place to start, just look at what you are clinging to the most tightly and start there. It's time to set yourself free!

32

KEEP YOUR GOALS
FROM THE TROLLS

Surround yourself with only people who are going to lift you higher.

~Oprah Winfrey

History has it that for centuries, fishermen have used a trick to catch a certain kind of crab that lives on the ocean floor. They lower a large basket down to the ocean bottom and crabs climb into it in search of food or shelter. Within a short period of time, there may be as many as a dozen or more crabs sitting in the bottom of the basket. The curious thing is that if one of them tries to climb out of the basket, the others grab it with their claws and drag it back down into the bucket. If that same crab is persistent and continues to try to lift itself out of the basket, the others pull it back down and rip its claws off. Eventually, the fishermen pull up the basket and have a feast!

The moral is obvious, isn't it? Many people have surrounded themselves with "crabs," those who do just about anything to hold others back, keeping them from lifting themselves up and out of a situation of limitation and moving into a better place in life. I suppose that this story supports the old adage "misery loves company." Sometimes it is easier to stay stuck in our limitations if we have others with whom we can commiserate, yes? The good new is that while the crabs in the basket can't do much about their situation, we can. We can choose the people with whom we will hang out. There are basically two types of people in life: lifter-uppers and puller-downers. We have a choice as to who we will be and whom we will call our friends. Is it easy to pull away from the puller-downers in our life? Of course not, because there is a huge power that comes from being part of a collective energy, even when it is negative.

So, where do we begin? We set some new goals for ourselves that take us in a new direction, placing us in an environment apart from those who are not lifter-uppers. And this is a vital point: Keep your goals from the trolls! Don't tell your plans to better your life to those who will try to discount your efforts and pull you back down. It may mean you hang out alone for a while, forcing you out of your comfort zone and creating an opportunity to make new friends. A great place to start may be your church or other service organization. Get involved with a group of people who are lifter-uppers, serving others. See how you too are lifted.

Mindfulness Practice

- Take an honest and unbiased look at the people you choose to associate with on a regular basis. Are they lifter-uppers or puller-downers? This is not an invitation to judge anyone. This is an opportunity to realistically discern where you are in your life and determine if you need to lift yourself up!

- After you have made your observation, if new goals are in order, write them down and share them with someone who you absolutely know is a lifter-upper.

- Remember, there is great power to be found in agreement, so be clear about those with whom you seek agreement.

33 DISCOVER THE REAL EIGHTH WONDER OF THE WORLD

People travel to wonder at the height of mountains, at the huge waves of the sea, at the long courses of rivers, at the vast compass of the ocean, at the circular motion of the stars; and they pass by themselves without wondering.

~St. Augustine

Like many others, I've gone to Hawai'i to "get away from it all," to seek the wonders of the world through nature, and to connect more deeply with spirit, which at times seems so difficult to do in the hustle and bustle of our day-to-day existence. On returning, I fully and humbly realize that I have just spent special time with some of the most beautiful, pristine, precious, sacred, serene, and amazingly unique expressions of God on the planet, all of which I felt deeply inspired by and spiritually connected with. I bet you think I'm referring to the stunning beaches, brightly colored birds, playful porpoises, majestic waterfalls, gentle trade winds, swaying trees, and plentiful plant life, but I'm not. While all those things also meet the description, what I found the most wondrous of all were the people I encountered on my sojourn. Other human beings! I ended up going to Hawai'i to have a spiritual epiphany about my relationship with other people! How wild is that? What I was trying to get away from became the high point of my journey.

What was it that caused this to happen? The spirit of generosity and authentic loving-kindness of those we met along the way was truly overwhelming. From our fellow travelers to our hosts and the local and native people we encountered at every turn—all seemed to embody what has been referred to as the Aloha spirit. The food servers in the restaurants, the airport personnel, the car rental representatives, the sales clerks, and the people on the street were extending themselves with what I chose to interpret as a sense of authentic joy, love, respect, and most important, reverence. Then, the most amazing thing happened. Upon my return home, I discovered the very same thing with the people in my own home, church, and community. Nothing had to change but my perception of life. The realization I had was that I didn't need to travel 2,500 miles to experience what I really went to Hawai'i for—to get away from the world by seeking beauty and peace in a distant land and culture. Granted, going there truly helped inspire me and realign my perspective, but the fact is that the real beauty in life lies within the hearts and souls of all the people we share our planet with, our family of the earth. The real peace we all seek lies in spiritually connecting with that family, not escaping from it.

When we lack the ability (awareness) to consciously look into other people's hearts and souls and feel that connection, we miss the opportunity to have a conscious relationship with God by means of Its highest form of expression, human beings. The saddest part is that we may also miss the real exquisiteness of life for if we can't see the authentic beautiful, pristine, precious, sacred, serene, and amazingly unique expressions of God in one another, we could sail the seven seas and seek the wonders of the world and would not find it there either. There it is, the real Eighth Wonder of the World, walking right by us every day: people! So don't miss the glory and wonder of it! As spiritual explorers, we know that's a treasure worth seeking.

Mindfulness Practice

⚜ Seek to spend some quiet time in the most beautiful spot you can find, where nature is at its pristine and peaceful best. With intention, feel the presence of spirit moving in, around, and through you. Notice the reverence you have for life and the sense of unity with the all dancing between you and your surroundings. It's very peaceful, isn't it?

⚜ Then, seek to spend some time with people with the sole intention of looking into them, connecting with their hearts and souls. Continue this practice until you can feel the same spirit moving in, around, and through you. Again, notice the reverence you feel for life and that sense of unity with the all dancing between you and those people. It's very peaceful, isn't it?

⚜ Realize that you have just had a mini-spiritual vacation, because in both instances, you have been basking in the beauty of the divine.

34   NEVER EVER GIVE UP!

*If I were asked to give what I consider the single
most useful bit of advice for all humanity it would
be this: Expect trouble as an inevitable part of life
and when it comes, hold your head high, look it
squarely in the eye and say, "I will be bigger than
you. You cannot defeat me."*

~Ann Landers

I am blessed and honored to have been invited to give an invocation
at the local opening ceremonies for The Relay for Life. This event is
sponsored by the American Cancer Society and has been held annually
for a number of years. Nationally, this event raises a considerable
amount of money for a very good cause. There is something else it
raises that is even more impressive: the spirit of hope, faith, and
courage of tens of thousands of individuals (and their families) who
have been or are afflicted with this life-threatening disease. Organizers
begin by raising a "tent city" for the weekend, which they call home.
What I witnessed was a community of friends and strangers coming
together to take a stand, united in their conviction that cancer will one
day not only be arrested but also be cured.

The amazing thing about this particular community is that they
come together to pray, grieve, and cry with one another as they
honor both loved ones and strangers who have passed on due to the
ravages of cancer. In addition, they come to be cheerleaders of sorts,
offering loving support and encouragement for friends and strangers
currently dealing with the disease. And finally, they come together to
play and celebrate life as they honor those who have fought the good
fight and won—the survivors of cancer. (I refer to them as victors.)
Honoring the survivors is a powerful thing to do because they are

living proof that there is good reason to keep the faith and stay emotionally strong. Just as our country has collectively taken a stand, looked terrorism in the face, and said, "You shall not have your way with us. We will never give up or give in to the tyranny of your terror," likewise cancer survivors have to have the courage to look into the face and terror of that disease and say the same thing. Does this mean that every person who never gives up will always win the battle with cancer or any life-threatening illness for that matter? Of course not, but statistics prove it's far more likely they will survive their ordeal with a positive attitude. There is something incredibly powerful about an attitude so full of resolve that it makes no room for compromises.

In his great book *Love, Medicine and Miracles*, Dr. Bernie Segal points out that the patients who most often survive cancer are the ones who are "uncooperative and difficult," the kind who are unwilling to blindly accept the opinions and take orders from their doctors without questioning them. They are the ones who look their problem right in the eyes and challenge its very authority over them. The mind is an amazingly powerful tool that can work for us or against us, depending on the altitude of our attitude. Combined with an awareness that the infinite intelligence of God always works through us at the level of our beliefs, it makes good sense to embrace a positive attitude and never ever give up. Believe in life, believe in the possibilities that lie ahead, and believe in the power of a supportive community . . . and then pass it on by celebrating The Relay for Life!

Mindfulness Practice

→ Draw the value from this lesson, as it is appropriate for you in your life today. Take a look at whatever is going on in your life that you may be feeling overpowered by or have given too much authority to and challenge it.

→ Look it in the eyes and tell it, "You shall not have your way with me . . . I will not give up . . . ever!"

→ If you need the support of a trusted friend, practitioner, minister, or therapist, by all means seek it.

35   USE IT OR LOSE IT

So you wish to conquer in the Olympic games, my friend? And I too, by the Gods, and a fine thing it would be! But first mark the conditions and the consequences, and then set to work. You will have to put yourself under discipline; to eat by rule, to avoid cakes and sweetmeats; to take exercise at the appointed hour whether you like it or no, in cold and heat; to abstain from cold drinks and from wine at your will; in a word, to give yourself over to the trainer as to a physician.

~Epictetus

Last weekend, our center had its annual picnic and softball game with a neighboring church. Between the 106-degree temperature, the softball game, and a spirited volleyball game, the day offered ample opportunity for exercise and to test the limits of one's body. (I was reminded of my body's limits that day.) The only time I ever play these sports is at this annual event. I must also tell you that the night before the picnic, Diane and I took our grandkids bowling, something I haven't done in thirty years. By Tuesday morning, my body was announcing to my mind the bad news: I hurt from stem to stern and everywhere in between! And, the worst part is, I do the same thing every year, hoping somehow I won't have to smell like Ben-gay for two weeks following the event. What's wrong with this picture? Obviously, I am asking my body to do things it has not been conditioned to do, and it's informing me that it doesn't like me doing that.

The message my body is sending me is simple: "If you want to play like a jock on the weekend, you have some work to do during the week!" Like everyone else, as I have "matured" physically, keeping my body in shape has become more difficult. It simply requires more time and effort than it did when I was eighteen, and therefore, not surprisingly, it has become less of a priority. As a matter of fact, whenever I have felt a sudden urge to exercise in the past few years, I have found that if I just lie down the feeling soon passes! It's amazing, isn't it? We can always find ways to avoid doing what we don't really want to do, even when we know it's for our own good.

What I have discovered for myself is that this truth extends far beyond my physical well-being. It is also true of my spiritual well-being. The fact is there is little difference between maintaining a fit physical body and maintaining a fit spiritual body. As Epictetus points out, "You will have to put yourself under discipline and take exercise at the appointed hour whether you like it or not." However, when that means doing our spiritual practices at 5:30 a.m., the temptation to just lie down is sometimes hard to resist, isn't it? The old adage "use it or lose it" comes to mind here. What we use grows stronger; what we ignore becomes weaker and begins to diminish until finally it has no energy to sustain itself. Irrespective of whether we are talking about our physical or spiritual bodies, use it or lose it seems to be the rule by which we must abide. So, what say you? Are you using your spiritual body daily? The daily exercises of reading, meditation, and prayer are essential to building strong spiritual muscles. Make no mistake about it, those muscles will make a world of difference as you enter into the arena of life to play the game each day.

Mindfulness Practice

➤ Take time today to examine what is important to you.

➤ If you discover that spirituality plays an important role in building and sustaining a life worth living, ask yourself if you are exercising your spiritual muscles properly and regularly. The answer will be somewhat obvious: If your practices are hit and miss, notice too that your life will reflect that energy.

➤ If you determine you need some assistance in building up your spiritual muscles, make a commitment to get to church more regularly, consider enrolling in classes that will help you develop those spiritual muscles and keep them fit, and/or hang out with people who will help you remember that your spiritual well-being is as vital to maintain as your physical body.

➤ Practice, practice, practice! And remember . . . use it or lose it!

36

A NEW WAY OF BEING HUMAN

*How do we surround that which is dying with
love?*

~David Whyte

If we are at all sensitized to what is really happening around our world, we will see that there truly is a new wave of understanding beginning to crest. This wave is rising to the call of a deeper compassion than we have ever known before. As this wave lifts us to a new perspective, we are being called to look beyond the trauma dramas with which the media are pummeling us. The old way of doing things is simply no longer working. In short, a large part of our culture and the belief system that has sustained it for so many years is changing. Metaphorically speaking, it's preparing to die, and a new culture, a new way of being human is preparing to be birthed. To echo the words of Lynn Twist, who spoke at the Association for Global New Thought conference in Palm Springs with great elegance and clarity, we must begin to understand that we are going to have to help hospice an old way of life that no longer works and midwife a new one that does.

I truly resonated with this statement when I heard it because I can identify with the metaphor. Hospice workers are among the most compassionate people on the planet because their sole (soul) job is to assist individuals through perhaps the most difficult thing anyone of us shall ever do, to die. They practice the art of deep compassion and loving-kindness and manage to do so without being swept into the emotions of it all. In short, their job is to assist those who are making their transition from one dimension of life to the next with as little pain and as much dignity and peace as possible. In many ways, this is what we are being called to do now with our culture. Today's quote by David Whyte poses the question so perfectly: How do we surround that which is dying with love? In recent days, I have heard much anger and resentment expressed toward those who represent a holding on to "the old way" of doing things. They may not support an evolving humanity be they in the corporate world, the political arena, and even in certain religious circles. As spiritually evolving individuals, we know that when someone is dying is not the time to find fault with him or her, irrespective of what they stood for. It's a time to assist the process with kindness and compassion. Likewise, this is the time to be mindful that we don't add to the pain we are all feeling by overreacting and being uselessly critical of the "old way" of being human, a way that is dying. Granted, this may be difficult to accomplish when the old way of doing things is making such a ruckus on the planet, gasping for its last few breaths. Regardless of the appearance, now is the time to take a God-sized step back and see it all through the eyes of a compassionate universe. It's about the evolution of our species, which includes each of us as well. Let us be sure that we are ushering in this new way of being human with reverence and gentle care for all—even those with whom we don't agree.

I consider myself to be a midwife to this new way of being human, which is in the birth canal right now. How about you? I believe we are preparing for the birth of a new kind of human, a conscious humanity that will openly know and celebrate the fact that we are all one in God, honoring our diversity and how we practice it. Will this all come to pass in our lifetime? Maybe, maybe not. But the contractions have already started, so we had better be ready to receive the baby with open arms.

Mindfulness Practice

To personalize today's message, take a look into your heart and see if there is any toxic emotion residing there for those who represent "the old way" of doing things. This can be in your own personal life or what you see going on globally.

First, imagine yourself as a hospice worker, assisting a dying person. How would you be there for that person? Of course, the answer would be, "With compassion and love for the spirit of God within the one who is transitioning." Can you see yourself in the same capacity now?

Second, imagine you are in the delivery room, working as a midwife, assisting in the birth of the most amazingly beautiful baby you have ever seen. Holding this baby in your arms, looking into its eyes, you realize that you are looking at every human being on the planet. How does it feel to hold the future of humankind in your arms? The truth is, you are doing so right now. A new way of being human begins with you and me. It begins with love and compassion for every being.

37

*I don't need to completely understand the big
picture to know that my role is important. I don't
have to know the destination to know I'm headed in
the right direction. Though I may not know where I
am going, I'm not lost, I am exploring.*

~Jana Stanfield

As my wife and I jumped into our rental car at the airport in Kona,
Hawai'i, we took a few minutes to study the map and directions
to our friend Mark's house. We were excited to be headed toward the
other side of the Big Island, which we were told was about a
two-and-a-half-hour drive. Well, after five hours of driving, we found
ourselves literally at a dead end. The one–lane road on which we were
traveling had been covered up some years earlier by a lava flow.
Clearly, we had turned left somewhere in the last one hundred and
thirty miles when we should have turned right. It seemed that we were
lost somewhere between the ocean, a whole bunch of lava, and a really
large jungle. We were on a one-lane road to nowhere. The sun was
setting, our cell phone had no reception, and it was beginning to rain.
At that point, things were starting to feel a bit tense. Then Diane looked
at me and in a most serious voice said, "Honey, we are at choice here
and we need to change our perspective." In the words of our friend
(and songwriter) Jana Stanfield, "Though we may not know where we
are going, we're not lost, we are exploring!" The longer we thought
about the wisdom of that statement the more we began to giggle, which
then erupted into an uncontrollable laughter. A slight shift in
perspective was all it took and our mistake instantly turned into an
adventure! We took a moment to pray for a shot of divine guidance and
then in the spirit of the adventure continued "exploring" the only other

road we could find in the darkness. Finally, we saw a light ahead that led us to a landline phone (located at what turned out to be a nudist camp), and Mark was on his way to rescue us. What an adventure that was!

So go our daily lives, yes? At one time or another, most of us have found ourselves thrust into an experience where we have felt lost (or at least out of control of the conditions), where the uncertainty of the outcome was a prevailing concern that kept us from fully being present in the moment. It doesn't have to be on a road trip, it could be in the midst of a job transition, a relationship, or a health challenge, or for that matter, even as one goes through the process of dying. It's easy to get lost in life, not knowing where we are going and, at times, feeling very much alone, isn't it? This is when we can choose to shift our perspective and see ourselves as "explorers." It has been said that in a confrontation between a stream and a rock, the stream always wins. It wins not because of its strength but because the stream is willing to explore new territory by simply surrendering to the call of gravity, flowing over, under, and around the rock in order to follow its purpose. A stream in time serves a larger purpose called river and, ultimately, ocean.

Just as the stream effortlessly follows the guidance and call of the law of gravity, you can rest assured that in those moments when you might feel lost in life, you have guidance calling to you as well. You just need to be open to it. It's actually the same intelligence, working at different levels. God's guidance is omnipresent, meaning that wherever you are, infinite intelligence is also. When you become willing to explore your experiences remembering this truth, especially in those moments of uncertainty, it sends a signal to the universe that you are receptive, open, and able to go with the flow. It's then that almost magically it seems, whatever guidance is needed to serve the purpose at hand is revealed with grace and ease.

Mindfulness Practice

- How willing are you to become an explorer? Are you willing to surrender to the lead of spirit?

- The next time you feel lost in life and without clear direction, first remember that in truth you can never really be lost. Lost is just a misperception based in a limited belief system that has you believing you are separate from God.

- Be open to the idea that you can never be separate from God but rather just exploring in God's grand allness.

- Invite your higher wisdom self to lead the way and trust the process by following spirit's lead. You will enjoy the journey far more. Who can say what other interesting things you may discover about your life along the way?

38

---

*The wise man builds his house on the solid rock of
Truth, and not on the shifting sands of instability.
He measures causes by effects and estimates Reality
by that which is real and enduring. The foolish
man, living only in sense perception, has no
measure for Reality and builds his home on false
and erroneous concepts; the vicissitudes of fortune
upset his frail building, the edifice falls about him
in ruins. Truth alone endures.*

~Dr. Ernest Holmes

The quote above by Ernest Holmes is obviously referring to the statement made by the teacher Jesus in Matt 7:24. In it, he gave his followers the parable of the man who builds his house on a foundation of rock, finding stability, whereas he who builds his house on shifting sand surely will see it crumble and fall. The rock, of course, is a metaphor for the truth that Jesus came to teach. The house is a metaphor for our lives. The truth Jesus came to teach us is universal in nature and is applicable to all human beings: "I and my Father are one." This is the truth about you and me as much as it is about this great teacher. When we build our lives on the solid foundation of this truth, our lives are unshakable and stable, able to withstand the gale–force storms of life. Shifting sand is a metaphor for an undisciplined mind, a mind that is focused on egoic needs (which change daily), a mind that thinks in terms of duality and the instant gratification that the material world promises and that is temporal at best. When we fail to build on the rock, we have chosen a building site right on the sandy beach. The view may be great for a while, but we discover it to be a very temporary home as it erodes right out from underneath us. Our lives end up becoming uncertain, shaky, and subject to the tumultuous events going on around us.

Several years ago, I was fortunate enough to purchase a new home, even before the foundation had been laid. I had the opportunity to watch it being built from the ground up. I watched the cement foundation being poured and I remember thinking how thick it was! Then I noticed that the post-tension slab was one large contiguous flow of cement and cables, which served as the solid foundation for every area, every room on the ground floor. There was no less cement being poured in the area that would be called "kitchen" than in the area that would be called "family room." The entire house was built on one solid foundation.

Do you get where I am going with this? If your life were a house, on what type of foundation would it be built? What would it look like? How many rooms would it have? What would they be used for, and how much time would you spend in each room? Think of the foundation as God's presence and think of each different room as the different aspects of your life. One room might be called "relationships," another room "physical health," another "work," yet another room "spirituality," and so on. When we are "awake," we realize that the same foundation supports every room equally. There is not more of God in one room than in another. When we are aware of this, every area of our life becomes solid and unshakeable. A life built on the foundation of the conscious awareness of God's presence in every "room" makes the entire house stable, strong, and able to withstand the storms and misfortunes to which we are all subject every day. It becomes a fit and joyful place to live. Building a consciousness of this awareness truly is building our house upon the Rock. Given the choice you have been given, where will you choose to build? It's never too late to move to higher ground!

Mindfulness Practice

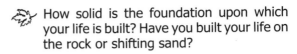 How solid is the foundation upon which your life is built? Have you built your life on the rock or shifting sand?

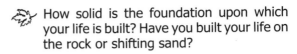 Take some time today as you analyze all the different "rooms" in your life, for example, relationships, work, health, creative expression, and so on.

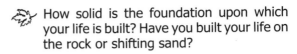 Become clear on how much of God's presence is realized in each of those rooms.

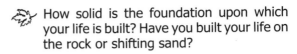 If you discover any imbalance or instability or if you feel like you are standing on shaky ground, make a commitment to yourself to begin drafting a new blueprint for your life.

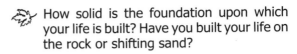 The key: Be sure the foundation is rock solid. Do what you have to do to put God first. Start now. Yes, NOW!

39

WHAT DEFINES YOUR WHOLENESS?

*We recognize that every form — from the smallest
quantum unit to the largest universal structure — is
engendered within the Wholeness of Spirit, and that
"in spite of all appearances" and behind such
images as disease and dysfunction, Spiritual
Perfection dwells. Such realization reveals to our
consciousness a more perfect state of being for
ourselves and others.*

~Stephanie Sorensen

One of the greatest quagmires in which new students of
metaphysics seem to get caught up lies in the mistaken idea that
wholeness manifests after everything in one's life is perfect. Of course,
the larger truth is that everything is already perfect in spite of those
times when our five senses might report to us a different reality. No
doubt, this can be a hard nut to swallow when we are enmeshed in a
painful physical or emotional condition that is privately screaming in
our inner ear "There's something missing here." For most of us, from
this state of consciousness, we believe "wholeness" is what's missing.
Somehow, we have mistaken wholeness to be a human condition at
which we will one day arrive. It's a place where there is no pain, no
challenges, no disease, no dysfunction, and no dark nights of the soul, a
place where there is nothing but peace, love, light, and pleasure. As we
mature spiritually, we learn it doesn't mean that at all. These are all
conditions that come as part of the human experience. As long as we
dwell in these garments of flesh and bone, we will be subject to the
human condition. Every master teacher I have ever studied has had to
contend with the aforementioned challenges. What did they know that
we have yet to learn? I recall, forever etched in my mind, the words

from one of my mentors, the late Dr. Fletcher Harding: "Wholeness is a state of being, not a condition." Being is another word for God's presence, manifesting in our experience NOW, irrespective of what it may look like to the world. The great teacher Jesus was saying the same thing when he admonished us to "judge not according to appearances, but judge ye with righteous judgment." Righteous judgment is simply seeing the truth at the center of all conditions; God is still there.

In my own experience, some of the most "whole" people I know are those who appear (to the judging eye) to be the most unfortunate and disadvantaged individuals. They may be dealing with a physical malady of some sort. It may be a life-threatening disease or simply an ongoing condition that renders them less than fully physically able. Irrespective of what it is, these individuals know a deeper truth about themselves, and because of that, they seem to radiate an inner peace and authentic joy. They refuse to be defined by their condition. Their wholeness comes from a deep remembrance of who they really are, which is of course God made manifest. God is not defined by the human condition. God is perfection being expressed in and though all of Its creation, in every holy instant. In other words, there is as much of God's perfection and presence in a cancer ward as there is in a fitness gym and health spa or, for that matter, even a sacred temple. More of God can't be in one place than another because God is All there is.

Spiritual perfection is an inherent part of each of us; it is never diminished by conditions. With an awareness of this truth comes the wholeness of spirit that enables us to accept the moment at hand as perfect, just the way it is, knowing that nothing is ever missing in God's presence. Our job is to cease judging by appearances and start knowing the truth. Will knowing the truth automatically change or fix that which we have previously labeled as imperfect? Understanding the power of an affirmative mind, it may. Even if it doesn't, it won't really matter because we will have ceased judging ourselves as well as others as less than whole. Wholeness is a natural part of the sacred continuum—that journey of spirit navigating Its way through the human experience as you and me. Know how blessed you are in this and every holy instant. It's all perfect in the eyes of God.

Mindfulness Practice

- Until now, how have you defined wholeness? Have you been waiting until conditions are perfect in your life before wholeness can be your reality?

- If so, take some time today to consciously refocus your perspective.

- Make a decision to cease judging by appearances and to no longer accept the opinions of others as your truth.

- Remind yourself that wholeness is a state of being, being one with God. That is the truth about you right now—you are one with God. Believe it, be It . . . and be whole.

40

THE POWER OF
GRATITUDE

---

*Gratitude unlocks the fullness of life. It turns what
we have into enough, and more. It turns denial into
acceptance, chaos to order, and confusion to clarity.
It can turn a meal into a feast, a house into a home,
a stranger into a friend. Gratitude makes sense of
our past, brings peace for today, and creates a
vision for tomorrow.*

~Melody Beattie

As a man told me the sad story of how life had been so unkind to
him, I listened not just to what he was saying but, just as
important, to what he was not saying. The perspective he held of his
life was indeed a negative one. I didn't hear one affirmative word come
out of his mouth. After about thirty minutes into our conversation, I
stopped him and asked, "If you could visualize your life as a glass,
would it be half empty or half full?" Without dropping a beat, he
replied, "Depends what's in the glass! If it is something bad, it is
definitely better than half full, and if it is something good, it's way
below empty." I recommended to him that he might want to have the
altimeter regulating the altitude of his attitude checked because he was
flying way below the radar screen of life. He asked me what kind of an
attitude I thought he should have, given the fact that his life is less than
wonderful. I suggested that if he were to work on developing an
attitude of gratitude, it would turn his life inside out.

In my work with people, I never cease to be amazed at how often
they tend to focus on what they don't have in life rather than the
incredible good they do have. It is not just folk wisdom that tells us
we should be focusing on the good in our lives now, it is
understanding the spiritual dynamics of a universe that only knows

how to increase the energy on which we focus our attention. The universe doesn't know or care if our glass is half empty or half full, that is a determination we make. However, an attitude of gratitude automatically brings with it a shift in consciousness that says, " I am open to receiving with a grateful heart." With that perspective, life has no alternative but to rush in and fill the glass with good.

In truth, there are actually two kinds of gratitude: the kind we feel for the good we receive and the more subtle kind we feel for the good we give. When we can enter into giving of our good to others with a sense of sincere gratitude for having it to give, it changes the entire dynamic of the experience for everyone involved. Simply put, gratitude changes our perspective of life. There is no better opportunity to practice an attitude of gratitude in our giving and receiving than now. This is a good time for all of us to reflect on the good in our lives regardless of how empty the glass may appear. Think about what Saint Paul encouraged us to remember: "In all things, give thanks." The truth is, if we look deeply enough, we will find blessings even in things and events that on the surface we might tend to judge as negative. In the process, notice your glass is getting fuller.

Mindfulness Practice

🖎 Begin a mindfulness journal, writing down everything in your life that you consider a blessing.

🖎 Need a place to begin? Is your heart beating? Do you have use of your legs and arms? Do you have two eyes that can see? As Thich Nhat Hanh would say, "Give thanks, even for your non-toothache." Do you have a roof over your head and did you have a meal today? Are there people in your life that care about you and who you love deeply? Do you live in a country where you are free and able to practice whatever religion you choose? I'm sure you get the idea.

🖎 Write in your journal daily for thirty days, rereading the entire journal every day for another thirty days and adding to it when led to do so.

🖎 In sixty days, check the altitude of your attitude of gratitude. In spite of all the challenges, you will see that life is essentially good. Be grateful for the gift of life and remind yourself often that God is the source of it all.

41   LIFE CYCLES

*There are cycles of success, when things come to
you and you thrive, and cycles of failure, when they
wither or disintegrate and you have let them go in
order to make room for new things to arise, or for
transformation to happen. If you cling and resist at
that point, it means you are refusing to go with the
flow of life, and you will suffer. It is not true that
the up cycle is good and the down cycle bad except
in the mind's judgment. Growth is usually
considered positive, but nothing can grow forever.
If growth, of whatever kind, were to go on and on, it
would eventually become monstrous and
destructive. Dissolution is needed for new growth
to happen. One cannot exist without the other.*

~Eckhart Tolle

I just returned from a stroll through my meditation garden, and I
experienced an awareness I want to share with you. At the time of
this writing, most of the flowers outside of my home are looking like
they are on the down side of their life cycle. They look tired, as if to say,
"OK, we have done our part to beautify your home, now we need a
break." By no coincidence, I just finished reading the above quote in
Eckhart Tolle's book *The Power of Now*. This quote reaffirms what I
had just experienced in the garden. It reminded me that the physical
experience really is one big cycle of up and down, ebb and flow, where
all living things are subject to the flow of life. I noticed that the flowers
in my meditation garden are not resisting the fact that their time is
coming to an end. It is only my judgment that says they are succeeding
more at being flowers in April, while in November they appear to be
failing in their purpose. At times, I think they seem to know more than I

do. I know from a spiritual perspective that the life force they really are does not end there. The body of the flower and the soil in which it grows and draws its sustenance is simply taking a time—out. In doing so, they make room for the new and unexpressed beauty yet to come in the spring.

This same metaphor can be used in many areas of our lives. The message is very clear. All that is has a beginning and an ending, where there is a period of rest (or restoration). Look around you. The planets have cycles, our bodies have cycles, day ends with night, night ends with day, summer ends with fall, fall ends with winter, winter ends with spring, and so on it goes around and around! I believe we tend to see the up as good and the down as bad. We need to look at this because without the down, there could be no up! The down prepares the way for the up. As far as our personal, emotional, and physical growth goes, there have to be some time—outs along the way or we would burn out. Those time—outs don't have to be perceived as down, but in truth that is what it is, isn't it? Down time? In the body of our relationships, there has to be some spaces of down as well as up—times to be alone so the relationship can breathe, finding balance and rest. Perhaps we have been clinging too long to a certain job when what may be needed is a time out for personal reevaluation and refocusing. How do we know when this is so? Listen to your heart and your body wisdom. Is it saying, "OK, I have done my part to enhance your life, it's time for a time out." Don't fear or resist the cycles of life calling you to take a time out. It is only natural. It is part of what we have come here to experience and be at ease with. Marvel at how your life cycles flow and honor them.

Mindfulness Practice

↪ Just as the sun is setting tonight, go outside and observe how it gently goes down over the horizon. No struggle, no fighting . . . just a quite settling into darkness.

↪ Notice how natural that seems. You have no fear or doubt that it will return again tomorrow to bring new light and life into your experience, do you? Just a deep let go. Think about the fact that as the sun sets here, it is rising elsewhere on this planet at the same time.

↪ Take time to review your personal life today and see where there may be any resistance to life as it cycles through the different dimensions of your life. Now, knowing that all of life is God in expression, let go, let God, and trust the process.

42   SURF'S UP!

You can't stop the waves, but you can learn to surf.

~Anonymous

Can you remember your first time at the beach when you stepped into the ocean and felt its awesome power in the form of the waves, swells, and undercurrent? At seven years of age and having just come from Ohio with little swimming experience in anything other than the YMCA indoor pool, I was somewhat intimidated by the roar, raw power, and vastness of it all. I saw the other kids out there just having a ball and I couldn't wait to try it, but I was not too excited about the temperature of the water or the size of the waves. However, I realized that if I wanted to play in the ocean I had to get wet and face the waves, so I jumped in. I recall wading out into the surf up to my neck and trying to keep my feet firmly planted on the sand under me as the waves and swells rushed toward me. As much as I resisted and fought the swells, they lifted me up off the ocean floor, and I floated like a cork on the water, totally out of control until the swell retreated and gently set me down again . . . until the next swell came. In time, I learned to cease resisting the waves and simply surrendered to them. I actually began to enjoy being lifted off of solid ground, and the feeling of being temporarily out of control was no longer a terrifying experience. It brought a certain sense of freedom and power with it; I felt sort of bonded with the power of the wave. It was an awesome feeling! This experience became one of my first life lessons, teaching me just how little control I really have over anything outside of my own mind and body and how vital surrendering my need to control is. I also discovered that learning to swim and ride the waves is a very experiential thing—we can't do it by watching others do it, we have to jump in and get ourselves wet. Life is just like the ocean, isn't it? Every day brings with it waves (challenges) and swells (fears larger than life) that seem to have so much power, and if we allow them to, they will intimidate us and keep us sidelined on the beach. However, if we want to have a fully expressed life, we are going to have to get wet and wade out into the surf. Yes, from time to time, we all have those waves that simply seem to overwhelm us. Those are the ones we need to be willing to be lifted by, not dragged under by. This can be difficult to do if we think we can control the waves. The key is to understand that we will never be able to control the waves of life, but surely, we can learn how to surf! It's about knowing how and when to let the waves lift us and carry us. It's about surrender in the moment and trusting that the divine intelligence within us knows what It is doing. If we are truly open to the lesson, each wave we encounter in life will contribute to making us master surfers—masters at letting go and letting God. As they say in Malibu, "Life's a beach and the surf is up," so jump on in and enjoy the ride.

Mindfulness Practice

At times, do you feel as though you are being overwhelmed by the waves in your life, being pummeled, tossed, and turned?

The next time you feel a wave coming on, notice any tendencies to try and push back or control the event or situation.

If you can clearly see that you are in over your head, in that moment of mindfulness, take a deep breath and invite the infinite intelligence that brought you into this world and sustains you to lift you and carry you over the condition and turbulence at hand.

Let go of any need to control or manipulate when in your heart you know you have no power to do so. Feel the sweetness of release and float in it with grace and ease. That is God, supporting you.

ARE YOU LIVING A LIFE OF SELF-BETRAYAL?

If your life includes things you profess to hate, yet you continue to do them anyway, that too, indicates self-betrayal. For example, are you always complaining about being overweight, yet you continue to be? Do you fail to exercise, go back to school, change jobs, confront your dead marriage, get a date, get a hobby, or deal with the pain of abuse or neglect that has scarred you since childhood? If so, you can't possibly be living in concert with who you were originally designed to be.

~Dr. Phil McGraw

Imagine that you have bought a brand–new computer and have just taken it out of the box. It comes from the manufacturer all shiny and fresh, with hardware and software that has been perfectly and purposefully designed specifically for that computer. Then over the years, you continue to add after-market hardware and software, which was never intended to be integrated with your system, including downloaded information off the Internet from total strangers. Pretty soon, you have a malfunctioning computer, but you continue to endure the problems because beyond the obvious inconvenience, you believe it is less costly in both time and money to live with the problems than it is to restore the machine to its factory specs. I know this can happen because I am describing my own experience.

So it is with life also: You and I came from the manufacturer all shiny and fresh, perfectly designed to be the authentic being God intended us to be. Then, over the years, we are downloaded with "programs" designed by others that cause our operating system to malfunction. Yet we continue to let these programs run long after we are aware that they don't really serve us well. Dr. Phil refers to this as living a life of self-betrayal. The obvious question we must ask is, Why would anyone choose to continue to betray themselves by living a life that is not only unrewarding but, in many cases, is downright miserable? Is their programming that powerful that they would choose to live in a manner that actually dishonors the authentic being they were originally designed to be? Of course, the answer is "yes," but it doesn't have to be that way. What does it take then to live a life in concert with who the Master Designer, God, originally intended us to be? It requires the willingness to reprogram ourselves, to delete all of the downloaded, erroneous information given to us by family, friends, and even strangers, which we mistakenly embraced as the truth about ourselves. It may require letting go of outdated "hardware" (e.g., relationships, jobs, addictions, habits, etc.) that do not serve us in living a life that honors the authentic being we were sent here to be.

This computer analogy works well for me because I can see how for the first thirty years of my life, I was operating with more than a few faulty programs and outdated pieces of hardware, which caused me to painfully live a life of self-betrayal. I share it with you, because if I can upgrade my "operating system," demonstrating a life of wholeness and inner peace that honors the divine designer, anyone can. When I have a computer problem I can't handle, I call on Jeff, my local computer wizard. When I have a challenge living in concert with who I came here to be, I call on a practitioner, minister, or a trusted friend who will help me remember who I really am. It is never too late to choose to be who you came here to be.

Mindfulness Practice

- If your life were a computer, what programs are you currently running? Take time today to review your beliefs and determine which ones honor your presence on earth and which ones don't.

- Ask yourself from where these "programs" came and begin to delete the ones that don't serve you in being who you were designed to be.

- Be sure that when you delete, you also add a new program titled "With God, All Things Are Possible."

44   SET YOURSELF FREE

*Although what you encounter and what you do in
each moment is appropriate and perfect to the
evolution of your soul, the shape of the experiences
of your life is determined nonetheless by the choices
you make. It is you that chooses to linger in
resentment, or to be consumed by anger, or
enveloped in grief, or to release these
lower-frequency currents of energy.*

~Gary Zukav

Isn't it amazing how life continues to put opportunities to heal right in our face, over and over again until we finally get it? After twenty-five years as a student of truth, I would like to think that I have mastered one of the basic practices, forgiveness, and the underlying foundation on which it is built, nonjudgment, but it whacked me upside the head while attending a minister's retreat. This was the second seminar in a matter of weeks that I attended, and clearly by no mistake, so did a particular peer of mine who many years ago, "did me wrong." (That's my story, of course.) I thought I had dealt with my resentment (judgment) long ago, but he showed up as a gift from the universe to assist me in seeing that I had not.

Because I had to share "sacred space" with him all week long, I discovered that I could not do my spiritual practice and at the same time hold him in contempt. The energy of resentment I held in my heart created a gap between me and God that was the size of the Grand Canyon. Plus, I felt hypocritical. I needed help bridging this gap. I have learned that when I ask God for guidance with a sincere heart, I had better be ready because it will show up. In my prayer work, I asked for assistance, and as they say, when the student is ready the teacher appears. One of the guest teachers at the retreat was the author of a new book by the title of—are you ready for this?—*Radical Forgiveness*. God not only comes through when asked, but He has a sense of humor too. In a workshop on forgiveness presented by the author himself, I had the opportunity (meaning in front of two hundred of my peers, I had no choice) to actually work face to face with this person who for years I had allowed to hold me hostage in a deep dark corner of my own mind. At that point, something amazing happened: As I looked directly into his eyes, I saw nothing less than God gazing back. It was at that moment that I was able to release this individual once and for all by seeing the gift he brought to me: the opportunity to experience God's presence in a new way. It was difficult to look beyond my history and in the holy instant of now experience love without conditions, without strings, and without the judgments I attached to how he conducted his life way back then . . . and now as well. Does this validate what he did so many years ago? Does it mean I wanted to hang with him like a new best friend? Of course not, it simply set me free from, as Gary Zukav says, "a lower frequency of energy" that was holding me in bondage in a prison of my own making. So, my encounter with him many years ago really was appropriate and perfect for the evolution of my soul. It helped me become a better lover of life—all of it—and I am healthier because if it. I had set myself free!

How about you? Are you allowing someone to keep you locked up in a prison of resentment, anger, or grief? If so, let this be the day when you set yourself free. You hold the key in your own hand; it is the key called forgiveness. It may even require radical forgiveness. The question is, Do you love yourself enough to use it? Irrespective of what has happened in the past, you can choose to use it for good, for the evolution of your own soul. Now breathe deeply and invite God to assist you in the process. Set yourself free today—you deserve it.

Mindfulness Practice

- Search your heart and see if there are any pockets of negative energy lingering around certain people or experiences in your past with which you may not have yet dealt. If needed, make a list.

- The first step may be simply acknowledging that there is a need to forgive. At this point, don't even try to do so. Simply ask God to lift you to a new perspective where you might be able to see the evolution being made available to your soul. From that perspective, you may find forgiveness easier.

- Then, let go and let God. Do it for you—set yourself free.

45

BE-CAUSE OF PEACE: PART ONE

Let there be peace on earth, and let it begin with me . . .

~Jill Jackson and Sy Miller

Upon my spiritual awakening in 1977, I discovered two profound truths that have become the centerpoint and foundation on which I have built and lived my life for the past twenty-seven years. The first truth is that God is all there is. The logic of this floored me because it meant that I am some part of what God is and that God is all of what I am. And the same is true about every other person on the planet. The second truth is that I live in a spiritual universe that operates on a law of cause and effect, creating my experiences in life by means of my use of it. This means that what is going on within me at the spiritual, mental, and emotional levels eventually manifests itself in my outer world in the form of conditions, events, and circumstances. At first, I was appalled by the idea that my life was the result (or effect) of my own making, because frankly, it wasn't all that pretty, and it was far less than peaceful. But I also began to see the power of this realization: If I was cause to my own effect, that meant I could change the effect by introducing a new cause! As simple as this awareness was, it radically altered my future.

With the new awareness of these two truths in mind, I began to understand why my daily life was in such a constant state of conflict, chaos, confusion, and pain. My body reflected this discord and so did the body of my relationships. As I began to apply my newfound truths to my daily life, I slowly became more and more aware that conflict, chaos, confusion, and pain were simply the effects of a mind that wasn't at peace with itself . . . mine! Shortly thereafter, I began to witness changes in my outer world that corresponded with the inner peace I was feeling. I made peace with my body and my relationships. Granted, in both cases, it required a willingness to release that which no longer served me in a healthy way. The fact is that manifesting any kind of peace (inner or outer) will require some form of deep letting go of our attachments to something. It could be something as ethereal as an idea, expectation, or resentment or something as tangible and material as real estate, money, or even a person or relationship. Letting go of what no longer serves you is a huge part of manifesting peace and, likewise, clinging a bit too tightly to anything will become cause to conflict, suffering, and pain. If you don't have an authentic sense of peace in your daily life, I encourage you to take a peek within and see what you might be hanging on to that no longer serves you.

Knowing that we are each but microcosms of the macrocosm, all I have shared with you regarding my personal experience could also be applied to world peace. Our world is no different from our personal lives. Peace on our planet will continue to elude us as a species until we make peace within ourselves. Indeed, as within, so without. And so, in her classic song "Let There Be Peace on Earth," Jill Jackson is right, it does begin with me. If I want to see peace in my world as a reality, I must first make peace with myself. I must first become that which I want the world to be. Amazing concept, isn't it? That is the challenge and the gift of this lifetime. So, how do we begin to make peace with ourselves? Tune in to the next message and find out.

Mindfulness Practice

☞ Make a conscious effort to breathe deeply with mindfulness. As you draw a deep breath in, hold it and ask yourself, "To what am I clinging too tightly today?"

☞ Listen without judgment. If you ask with sincerity and you listen with an open mind and heart, you will hear exactly what is calling you to become the cause of your own experience of peace.

☞ As you release your breath, see yourself releasing whatever came forward in your awareness. Notice as you become more at peace, you add that energy to the planet too. That's a good start, yes? Be-cause . . . of peace.

46

THE NAMASTE
DAISY CHAIN:
BE-CAUSE OF
PEACE, PART TWO

*The same stream of life that runs through my veins
night and day, runs through the world and dances
in rhythmic measure.*

~Rabindranath Tagore

In the previous message, after stating that we must first become what we desire the world to be, I posed the question, "How do we begin to make peace with ourselves?" As I pondered this question, I was overwhelmed with the complexity and the simplicity of it. It is as simple as understanding the first truth of which I spoke, which is that God is all there is. It is also as difficult as remembering to remember this first truth. We have forgotten what we intrinsically knew as newborn babies: We came from pure spirit and still are pure spirit. We are each individuated spiritual beings, swimming in the common essence of one spirit, God. It was when we put on these spacesuits of flesh and bone that we began to believe in the illusion that we were separate from one another, and God. I believe that most turmoil and absence of inner peace is caused by an underlying (and most often unconscious) sense of detachment: a fear of being alone and apart from the wholeness of life. Of course, a lack of inner peace by enough individuals leads to a lack of world peace.

The obvious answer to making peace with ourselves is simple: Reveal the presence of God within and without, dissolving all sense of separation from It. A realization of our spiritual wholeness intrinsically brings with it inner peace because we realize in God's presence that we lack nothing. Then we are free to extend that sense of our own sacred wholeness to our world without reservation. As humankind moves into a conscious awareness that all human beings are interconnected at the level of one spirit, a realization of our wholeness as a species will prevail, and the energy that sustains the illusion of separation will vanish. At that point in our evolution, harming one another will be an unthinkable act because we will understand that to do so would only be harming oneself. The question is, How do we bring this awareness to our world?

In 1977, as I began to spend time with people who I considered to be spiritually grounded, I would often hear them saying the word "Namaste" (Na-ma-stay) to one another. Then, with hands held in a prayer position, they would offer a slight bow, given as a sincere sign of reverence for one another. Namaste comes from the ancient language of Sanskrit and it means "I honor the place in you in which the entire universe dwells. I honor the place in you that is love—of truth and peace. When you are in that place in you and I am in that place in me, we are one." A shortened Westernized version of the definition for Namaste might be "The divinity in me honors the divinity in you." I like the idea that one word, when embodied, can speak so loudly that no lengthy definition or superfluous words are needed. When I observe someone who understands the true meaning of Namaste, it becomes obvious to me that the word provokes a deep sense of inner peace, great reverence, for another, and loving-kindness. Can you see it? This is where the second truth of which I spoke in my last writing comes in: The sacred act of honoring God's presence in oneself and other people manifests as inner peace and thus becomes the cause. Reverence and acts of loving-kindness are the resulting effects. Then, in turn, reverence and acts of loving-kindness become cause to the effect we call peace between individuals. This peace between individuals then becomes cause, which leads to the effect of peace between nations. It is sort of like a Namaste daisy chain, continually unfolding from within each individual to another and outward to the world.

This Namaste consciousness might well serve as the catalyst for world peace. Could it be as simple as teaching the world's next generation the meaning and use of one simple word? The word isn't really that important because it is just a symbol. We know that words themselves have no power; the power to transform comes from the intention, feeling, and conviction behind the word. Saying Namaste to others would be useless unless we can first look into the mirror and say it with sincere reverence and loving-kindness. What better place could there be for world peace to start than the mirror? The word is Namaste—spread the word!

Mindfulness Practice	
	Make a commitment to live in a true Namaste consciousness for the next seventy-two hours. Practice the presence of God with such intensity that you feel marinated in God's love for Itself, by means of you.
	Then, extend that love to others and the world. As within, so without.
	Notice that you are becoming cause to the effect of peace. That's how powerful your consciousness is, and how necessary it is for this planet's future.

47 GROW DEEP AND STAND TALL

The greater the contrast, the greater the potential.
Great energy only comes from a correspondingly
great tension between opposites.

~C. G. Jung

There was a great experiment done in the early 1980s in the desert called the biodome. It was an exercise to create the perfect living environment for human beings, plant, and animal life. A huge glass dome was constructed and an artificial, controlled environment was created with purified air and water, filtered light, and so on, offering the perfect growing conditions for trees, fruits and vegetables . . . and humans. People lived in the biodome for many months at a time, and it was wonderful because everything seemed to do well, with one exception. When the trees that were planted grew to be a certain height, they would simply topple over. It baffled scientists for the longest time until one day they realized the one natural element they forgot to recreate in the biodome: wind! Trees need wind to blow against them, which in turn causes their root systems to grow deeper into the soil, which in turn supports the tree as it grows taller.

What a great lesson we can take from the biodome experiment. Who among us doesn't long for a perfect growing environment with no disruptions from outside influences? We strive to avoid the times of contrast and tension, those times when the challenges of daily life push against us. When they do, the normal tendency is to curse them. If the trees could talk, I wonder if we would hear them curse the wind each time they encountered a storm. I doubt it very much. More likely, I believe we would hear them thank the wind for assisting them in deepening their root system, enabling them to grow stronger and taller. That's nature's wisdom at work.

We can learn a great deal from the nature of a tree if we are open to the lesson. Watch how a tree bends and sways gracefully when the wind blows against it. It does not stand rigid, resisting the flow of energy. It does not push back. The tree accepts the strong wind as a blessing that helps it grow. Like a tree, we too need the contrast of the winds of life pushing against us. In those times, we need to remember that God is the soil, the essential foundation upon which we grow our lives. Then we can view the challenges in our lives as blessings. It is that contrast that develops our character and deepens our spiritual roots in the soil of God's presence and power. Be flexible . . . bend and sway with the wind. Grow deep and you will stand tall.

Mindfulness Practice

- Take a look at your challenges, those times of contrast you may currently have blowing as gale–force winds in your life and give thanks for them. See them as the wind . . . and see yourself as a tree.

- Then turn to the source and deepen your roots into the truth. Those are the times when our taproot draws its life force from the creator.

- There is no such thing as a perfect life. If there were, we could not survive in it. Be thankful it is so.

48

*Don't be afraid to make a mistake, your readers
might like it.*

~William Randolph Hearst

One of the ways I try to affect people in a positive way is to write and send an e-mail message a day to a list of subscribers. In fact, that daily e-mail is the foundation for this book! I am uncertain of just how many of my e-mail subscribers were bombarded with one of my messages recently. I understand that some people received it as many as forty times! Clearly, there had been a mistake made by one of the technicians who maintains our website, and I extended my deepest apologizes for any inconvenience it may have caused my readers. Out of about a thousand subscribers, I received a good number of responses informing me of the problem. Most of them were lighthearted, a few of them were very "expressive" of their discontent over the inconvenience it had caused, and several even asked to unsubscribe. It is amazing how life continues be a magnificent mirror, reflecting back to us exactly that which we project. To this, I quote Nelson Boswell, who wrote, "The difference between greatness and mediocrity is often how an individual views a mistake." At first, even I was more than a bit upset with our web manager. Then, one morning at four o'clock, I got it! My view shifted: This wasn't about him; it was about my reaction to his "mistake." This has been an interesting opportunity for me to practice what I preach. I invite you to see what value it holds for you as well.

The problem happened because I had requested the website manager to seek a new method so that the daily e-mail message could be sent out more efficiently. In other words, there would have been no problem at all if I had been willing to continue doing things in the manner in which they had always been done. However, what I have discovered over the years is that if I always do what I have always done, I will always get what I have always gotten. It's not my way to settle for mediocrity if a better way to do something can be discovered. The operative word here for me is "discovered."

Too often, we choose to settle for the status quo because of the risk involved with new discoveries. We fear we may make a "mistake" venturing outside our box (current reality) and so we settle in for the long run, living our lives with an inner knowing that there is something greater awaiting us beyond our comfort zone. It woos us, inviting us to move forward into the unknown where anything is possible, including making mistakes . . . so we hold back. The belief is that mistakes are a bad thing. The fact is that a person who has never made a mistake has never tried anything new. Yes, it is safer not to make any mistakes, but that means we have to live small, restricted, redundant, and unrewarding lives, which is not what you and I were sent here to do. We have been sent here to grow and evolve consciously, to expand our horizons. A fear of making mistakes drastically limits those horizons, doesn't it?

Well, it's easy to stop making mistakes: Just stop having ideas, stop growing, stop living. If you don't find this an unacceptable choice, then I invite you to take a step out of your comfort zone and welcome your mistakes. It is proof you are alive! So, I am glad that our web manager made the mistake—it wasn't his first and I pray it won't be his last. It's proof he is doing his job, seeking new and better ways that allow me to connect with you more efficiently. Our mistakes can be the bridge between inexperience and wisdom. May each bridge you cross be meaningful to you on this amazing journey called life. It's all good!

Mindfulness Practice

How tolerant are you of the mistakes you make?

How about the mistakes others make?

Take some time today to think about how you have viewed mistakes up until now. Perspective is everything. A new awareness can change your experience. For example, making mistakes can be an amazing gift. Perhaps the next mistake you make will be the one that opens you up to your own greatness. Welcome your mistakes—it's proof you are growing.

49

TAKE A GLOBAL VIEW

If we could, at this time, shrink the Earth's
population to a village of precisely 100 people, with
all existing human ratios remaining the same, it
would look like this: There would be 57 Asians, 21
Europeans, 14 from the Western Hemisphere
(North and South), and 8 Africans. Seventy would
be non-white; 30 white. Seventy would be
non-Christian, 30 Christian. Fifty percent of the
entire world wealth would be in the hands of only 6
people. All 6 would be citizens of the United States.
Seventy would be unable to read. Fifty would suffer
from malnutrition. Eighty would live in
sub-standard housing. Only 1 would have a college
education. When one considers our world from
such an incredibly compressed perspective, the need
for both tolerance and understanding becomes
glaringly apparent.

~Forest Felling

While I can't vouch for the accuracy of the statistics quoted above, I do believe it's of profound importance that we embrace the essence of the message. It's interesting to note that most of us reading this message are probably in the minority according to these stats. Think of it: If you can read and write and have a full stomach each night when you lay your head on your down-filled pillow in your heated home with carpeting on the floor and a car or two in the garage, you are in the minority. And if you are educated beyond the high school level, you are truly among a very few. Granted, all of this is from a global perspective, which makes it all the more meaningful.

I think that for those of us born in the West, the tendency is to take much for granted—so much so that perhaps the amazing amount of good we have managed to manifest in our lives has blocked our view of what life really looks like for the majority of our brothers and sisters in our Earth family. It's easy to become just a bit jaded when life is so consistently good, isn't it? This is not to say that we don't also have an abundance of serious challenges right in our own country, towns, neighborhoods, and homes because truly many of us do. But still, when compared with how the majority of the world exists, we can see that we are blessed beyond measure.

This isn't about feeling guilty for how good we may have it, because we all deserve every ounce of good we have manifested in our lives. It's about feeling so fully connected to life that it causes us to live each day with a mindfulness not to take any part of it for granted. With such present moment awareness, the extraordinary amount of good we do have tends to then overflow, spilling into the lives of others in amazing ways. Can you imagine the impact it would have on the world if the "minority" lived with such mindfulness? My message today is simply an invitation to take a few minutes out of your day and see the bigger picture. While you and I may be in the minority from a global perspective, the majority of the world can benefit greatly from our sense of connectedness to the whole.

Mindfulness
Practice

Take a look beyond your own life, beyond your own good, extending your view to include the entire planet: See how the rest of the world is doing. This exercise will help create a true feeling of humility, and it may also foster a new sense of tolerance, understanding, and compassion for a world in which daily pain and suffering is normal.

Then take some form of action to extend yourself to that world in a manner that makes a difference.

At the very least, include every human being in your prayers, wishing for them the very same good you desire for your most cherished loved ones.

Get involved, not because you should but because you can.

50

WHAT DO YOU LOVE?

Attention is a tangible measure of love. Whatever receives our time and attention becomes the center of gravity, the focus of our life. This is what we do with what we love: We allow it to become our center. What is at the center of your life? Carefully examine where you spend your attention, your time. Look at your appointment book, your daily schedule . . . this is what receives your care and attention — and by definition, your love.

~Wayne Muller

To a large degree, who we are is defined by what we love. What do you love? If you take this question seriously, it will not only help you clarify what your priorities are, but it will help you see who you are. If you can remain honest with yourself, you may discover that sometimes it is appropriate to stop and recalibrate those priorities. Place them in a new order, an order that transcends the needs of the head and focuses on honoring the needs of the heart and spirit, which quite often seem to get pushed to the bottom of the priority list. While it may not always be pleasant, it is easy to determine whether a recalibration of your priorities is in order. As Wayne Muller states, take a look at what is at the center of your life. Where do you spend your precious energy and time? Where is your attention focused? This is where that which you actually love resides. Granted, it is easy to come up with many good, logical reasons why our priorities are the way they are. I have heard them all, and frankly at times I've tried a lot of them too. A few prime examples might be "Without this job I spend so much of my life at, I wouldn't be able to support my family" or "I've got to get out on that golf course every weekend, because I have too much stress from my job, which I spend all my time at" or "I can't get up early enough to get to church on Sunday because it's my only day off, and I am tired from playing golf and poker on Saturday" or "I would get to the gym and exercise, taking care of my health and honoring my body temple, but I have to get to work!" On and on and on the cycle goes unbroken. My point is this: Is it wrong to "love" our work, recreation time, and our individual pursuits, which seem necessary to keep on keeping on? Of course not. If anything, let's hope we do love those things greatly but not at the expense of our core values, that which truly makes us whole. What makes us whole, really? A good place to start may be our relationships: first and foremost, the relationship we are having with life and the God of our being and, second, the relationship we are having with ourselves, our family, and our friends. The challenge we seem to face as a culture is that we tend to get caught up in the external pursuits in life, and our priorities become distorted. The doing, getting, and achieving become more important than the being, being one with God and being present with our loved ones. If this rings a familiar bell, perhaps it is time to reexamine your priorities. What do you love, really? Just look at the center, the hub of your life, and you will know.

Mindfulness Practice

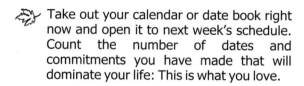 Take out your calendar or date book right now and open it to next week's schedule. Count the number of dates and commitments you have made that will dominate your life: This is what you love.

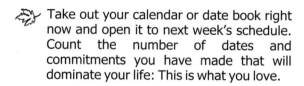 If what you love reveals a center (or focus) with which you are happy and are pleased to call the core of your life, congratulations!

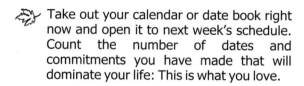 If it doesn't, don't despair. Simply call forward the awareness that you can choose to set new priorities, beginning today.

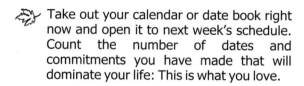 Where do you begin? Listen to your heart, it will tell you exactly what your priorities need to be. Life is quite wonderful when we honor what we love by consciously making it the center of our lives. This can never happen until we are crystal clear on our priorities.

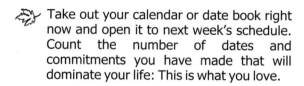 Tomorrow never comes, so do it now!

51

DIVINE SURRENDER: YOUR DEFINING MOMENT

Father, if Thou art willing, remove this cup from Me; yet not my will, but Thine be done.

~Luke 22:42

I believe that the experience Jesus had in the Garden of Gethsemane just prior to his arrest and subsequent crucifixion was his true, divine-defining moment. That was the moment he actually became the Christ, as his egoic self finally and totally gave way to his pure spiritual essence. He had made the divine surrender, fully giving his spirit, mind, and body back to God. In this surrender, any and all sense of separation from God was dissolved. Up until that point, the human Jesus was struggling with the Christ Jesus. In Luke 22:44, it is written, "And being in agony he was praying very fervently; and His sweat became like drops of blood, falling down upon the ground." Drops of blood is a metaphor depicting the fact that he was deeply enmeshed in fear. Who can blame him, for he knew what he was about to go through. This was an entirely understandable reaction for any human being to have. But, this is also where the human gave way to the divine.

If we read the rest of the story, we notice that from the moment Jesus made the divine surrender through the moment of his crucifixion, fear, anxiety, and uncertainty were no longer a part of his reality. Even as he stood before Pilate, when asked if he was the king of the Jews, his response wasn't one of someone coming from fear. He calmly said, "It is as you say." He had no need to argue, deny, or defend, because in his defining moment his true identity had been realized and he knew who he really was. Who Pilate said he was didn't matter. From that place of divine knowing, only peace remained as his experience.

I don't know about you, but I have been in my own Garden of Gethsemane more than once. Perhaps not where I was facing imminent physical death, but who says we have to be facing the loss of our life to be sweating drops of blood? Whenever we are overcome with fear, it is always attached to a concern of loss at some level. Perhaps it's the loss of a relationship or loved one, a material possession, a job, a reputation, or _____ (fill in the blank). Whatever the perceived loss, making the divine surrender will always be the answer. "Not my will, Father, but Thine be done." This demands that we let go of our need to control the universe, doesn't it? It's always about the lesser giving way to the greater and our willingness to be the vessel though which it may happen. Remember this: God's will is quite simple. It only seeks a bigger part of your life through which It may have fuller expression, revealing more of Its divine self. In the process, we may have to make peace with the fact that something we have been clinging to must be released. This can be a very personal and difficult thing to do, but it is how we make way for the greater expression of the divine through us and as us. Our true defining moment then is when we open to this awareness and give way to it. At that moment, as Jesus did, we will know ourselves as God moving through the human experience, regardless of how dark it may appear to be to others. The next time you are having a Garden of Gethsemane experience, try to remember that it could be your defining moment to reveal who you really are . . . to yourself and the world.

Mindfulness Practice

⧽ What is God's will for you?

⧽ It takes great courage to make the divine surrender, but it is the only way to create that opening through which God may show up in ways that will transform your life.

⧽ Explore those areas where your ego (EGO = edging God out) seems to be clinging too tightly. It's very likely that is where the release process must begin.

⧽ Now, take a big breath and say with me, "Not my will, God, but Thine be done." Yes, you may need to do this 777 times a day, but just think about it, you are having a divine-defining moment.

52

FREE AT LAST!

I have decided to stick with love. Hate is too great a
burden to bear.

~Dr. Martin Luther King, Jr.

Hate is a toxic energy that can wear many different masks, but behind them all dwells the same thing: fear. Have you ever carried the burden of hate? I have, and I know how hard it is to let it go. It is particularly difficult when it seems to be justified because of someone else's act of cruelty, thoughtlessness, or selfishness. Irrespective of how or why the hate shows up, when we are stuck in our emotional body with intense feelings of hate, we are the ones who suffer the most because we isolate ourselves from life and actually end up holding ourselves a hostage from happiness.

Sadder yet is the burden of hate in which many people are immersed without even realizing it because their caretakers taught them hate as a way of life, even before they could talk. There is no question that this kind of hate is born in the fertile womb of fear, which most often shows up as an overinflated sense of superiority, intolerance, bigotry, and arrogance. This is sad because it really boils down to a lack of understanding others who may be different than they are, and in general, ill-informed people tend to fear what they don't understand. When lack of understanding commingles with fear, it becomes a recipe for hate, and too often it shows up in some form of violence. This is the lesson that Dr. Martin Luther King, Jr. brought to light in an amazing way in the 1960s. It was the beginning of a new page in the book of the evolution of humanity.

There is yet another point of origin for hate and that is self-hatred—it often comes with the fear of not being enough. This kind of hate originates from a deep feeling of inadequacy, which is then projected outward onto a convenient target. The ego would much rather we focus our hate outward than inward. No matter how we slice it, hate is fear in drag. It's a huge burden to bear for our entire lives, isn't it? Regardless of how it came about, if hate is a burden we bear today, we owe it to humankind, to our friends and family, and more important, we owe it to ourselves to heal it. Why? Because life is not too short, it's too long to live it in a self-imposed bondage, and it doesn't serve our soul's purpose. We can't express the glorious being we came here to be while staying stuck in the energy of fear and hate.

The good news is, we don't have to bear hate any longer. We can set ourselves free today. How? Of course, Dr. King was right . . . stick to love. Easier said than done? Sure it is! It is much easier to fear than to love because fear seems to be the way of the world (up until now). If it were easy, everyone would be at peace with themselves and others. That's not the case yet——but it's not impossible. If we feel the burden of hate weighing heavy upon our heart, we can invite that place within us where divinity dwells to take over. Just remember, in Its highest vibration, God is love. Give your hate (fear) up to God and watch it dissolve. Hate exists in the darkness of duality and a sense of separation from the light. Just as darkness cannot exist in the presence of light, fear cannot maintain its existence in the presence of love. Stick with love and be burden free.

Mindfulness Practice

Even if you believe you have no energy around the issue of hate, take an emotional and mental inventory today and determine if there are any hidden pockets of fear hiding out somewhere in the cracks between your thoughts and feelings. Oftentimes, hate will disguise itself as intolerance, superiority, and more subtle toxic emotions such as inferiority.

If you discover this is true for you, it may be time to let go and let God. Try it, and notice how free you feel.

53   EVERYWHERE I LOOK

My religion is very simple – my religion is kindness.

~Dalai Lama

Have you ever had someone say or do something to you that was cruel and unkind? I have. Some of my best teachers have been unkind people who have helped me feel the pain that can be caused by thoughtless words and actions. They have also helped me see that part of myself that can sometimes be unkind.

If you take time and observe people who you might consider spiritually enlightened, you will notice an inherent energy of reverence and loving-kindness accompanying their words and actions. They seem to have embodied what loving-kindness really means. Is there a connection between their relationship with God and the relationship they are having with other people? I think so.

In the East, loving-kindness is considered a spiritual practice, part of what becomes a person's deep character. How can we move more closely toward building a consciousness of loving-kindness? Repeat this mantra to yourself, "Everywhere I look, I see the face of God." When we begin to see the divinity within every individual, how could we not treat that person with respect and loving-kindness? Is this easy to do? Of course not, especially when we realize that those we tend to unconsciously treat unkindly (or who treat us unkindly) may be those closest to us. They often serve as a mirror, reflecting back to us some aspect of our own character that needs to be more fully loved. That is why the Dalai Lama called kindness his religion . . . it takes discipline and commitment to practice. Start a new religion for yourself today. Be kind to yourself and others—it could catch on!

Mindfulness Practice

- As you share this day with others, choose to be hypersensitive to the degree of respect you extend to them even if by means of their actions you have concluded (judged) they don't deserve your respect.

- The truth is, at the center of every living being dwells a living Christ. This sacred presence awaits our recognition of it. Respecting and honoring the divinity in others calls us to act with loving-kindness toward everyone.

- What makes this exercise even more meaningful is when you realize that by treating everyone else with kindness, you are really being kind to yourself. If God is all there is, it can be no other way.

54

IT'S A BEAUTIFUL DAY IN THE NEIGHBORHOOD

We live in a world in which we need to share responsibility. It's easy to say, "It's not my child, not my community, not my world, not my problem." Then there are those who see the need and respond. I consider those people my heroes.

~Fred "Mister" Rogers

As I sat eating dinner with my eighteen-year-old daughter last night, she shared with me that she had just volunteered to be a mentor in the Big Sister program with Interface, a community service organization. I silently swelled with pride as once again my "little girl" gave me a peek at the compassionate soul she came here to share with the world. I am humbled by her grace and ability to be so clear on her priorities at such a tender age. I reflected on what may have nurtured this compassionate soul to reveal so much of itself so early, when many her age are more concerned with whether they will have a date on Friday night.

It was in that moment of contemplation that I remembered one of the daily rituals she and I shared together from the time she was about a year old. I flashed back to 1986 and remembered how we sat together every morning and watched *Mister Roger's Neighborhood* on television. We continued this practice until she was about seven years old. We also watched *Sesame Street*, which was great for learning words and simple math skills, but what Fred Rogers was able to convey to children went far beyond good grammar and addition. He taught his TV family of children (and a few of us older kids) how to experience our emotions and feelings. He made it okay for kids to be happy or sad, and he taught us how to deal with those feelings in a proactive and healthy way. To quote him, "Of course, I get angry. Of course, I get sad. I have a full range of emotions. I also have a whole smorgasbord of ways of dealing with my feelings. That is what we should give children. Give them ways to express their rage without hurting themselves or somebody else. That's what the world needs."

It was his willingness to live and teach from his own sense of connectedness to life and others that taught us the true meaning of friendship, generosity, kindness, and yes, compassion. Truly, the world needed what Mister Rogers shared with us for several generations, and it still does. Fred Rogers passed to the next dimension on his eternal spiritual journey on Thursday, February 27, 2003. Wherever that may be, we can rest assured that the neighborhood in which he lives is a better place because of his presence there. There is no doubt in my mind that some part of Mister Rogers lives within the heart and soul of my grown daughter today and that those whom she will serve for many years to come will benefit directly from the time she spent hanging out in a certain neighborhood so many years ago. Here's to you Mister Rogers. Thank you for making a difference in my life, my child's life, and God only knows how many other lives. Thank you for making the world a better place . . . a place in which a kid may be a healthy and happy kid, because as I have learned, healthy and happy kids grow into healthy, happy, and compassionate adults and that's what our world needs a whole bunch more of now.

Mindfulness
Practice

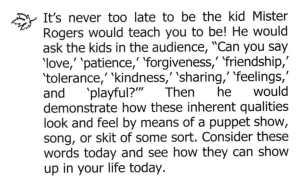 It's never too late to be the kid Mister Rogers would teach you to be! He would ask the kids in the audience, "Can you say 'love,' 'patience,' 'forgiveness,' 'friendship,' 'tolerance,' 'kindness,' 'sharing,' 'feelings,' and 'playful?'" Then he would demonstrate how these inherent qualities look and feel by means of a puppet show, song, or skit of some sort. Consider these words today and see how they can show up in your life today.

If it will help, consider it a spiritual practice, because that's exactly what it is. These are but a few of the qualities by means of which a spiritually evolving being expresses his or her true nature. It really is a beautiful day in the neighborhood, isn't it?

55

HE WHO LAUGHS...
LASTS!

Laughter is the sun that drives the winter from the human face.

~Victor Hugo

There was once a group of friars who were behind on their belfry payments so they opened a small florist shop to raise funds. Since everyone liked buying flowers from men of God, a rival florist across town thought the competition was unfair. He asked them to close down but they refused. So the rival florist hired Hugh McTaggart, the biggest, toughest thug in town to "persuade" them to close. He beat up the friars and trashed their store, saying he'd be back if they didn't close down. Terrified, they did indeed close, proving that Hugh and only Hugh can prevent florist friars.

A bit corny, yes, but I'll bet it made you crack a smile and hopefully laugh too. Most of us tend to take much of life far too seriously, especially in those times when we have no immediate control over our circumstances. This is not to diminish the challenging times to which we are all subject but rather to consider how fear and stress affect our well–being, and equally, how joy and laughter can affect us. I believe we tend to forget about the amazing healing power that can accompany heartfelt laughter and joyous and kindhearted humor. The fact is that when we are immersed in a good belly laugh, we tend to be so fully present in the moment that we forget about anything and everything else. The past and the future seem to momentarily dissolve into nothing, and the joy of being in that holy instant is all there is. This is why children laugh far more often than adults. They are more fully present in the moment because they are not consumed with what tomorrow "may" bring or with the regrets of yesterday. Deep laughter is sort of like a minivacation for our minds, which of course has everything to do with what's going on in our bodies. From a medical perspective, it has been proven that humor and laughter play a vital role in expediting the healing process. In his best-selling book, *Anatomy of an Illness*, Norman Cousins professes to have demonstrated a total physical healing from a crippling disease by watching nothing but movies of the Marx Brothers and the Three Stooges for a prolonged period of time. He says, "Laughter is inner jogging." It's true! When we laugh, our insides get a great workout. Endorphins and other health-stimulating chemicals are instantly and automatically pumped into our bloodstreams, and our bodies receive the relaxing and healing benefit from it. Somebody said that laughter is the only tranquilizer that has no harmful side effects.

From a spiritual perspective, we are always seeking ways to connect and share our sense of unity with God and other human beings at a deeper level. When you consider it, laughter can really dissolve the distance between people because our hearts all speak the same language. Irrespective of the language or the culture, a sincere laugh is unmistakably understood. When people laugh together, it's because in that moment, they are sharing something in common, a moment of feeling the same thing, which is when boundaries disappear. This is how authentic peace begins. Perhaps Mark Twain said it best: "The human race has but one really effective weapon, and it is laughter." When you think about it, when we laugh together, it can be disarming, can't it? So, whether we are talking about inner peace or world peace, more laughter could be just what we need. We all have a vital role to play in this process. It's crucial that we work together with humility, so I close with these words of wisdom: Remember that those who get too big for their britches will be exposed in the end! <Smile> More than anything else, just remember, he who laughs . . . lasts!

Mindfulness Practice

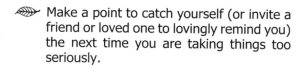 Make a point to catch yourself (or invite a friend or loved one to lovingly remind you) the next time you are taking things too seriously.

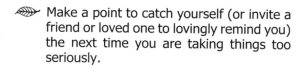 Take a deep breath and then look for something in which you can find humor. Perhaps you can keep a joke book or comic strip in your desk drawer or glove box or turn your TV on and watch *Comedy Central*. Try standing on your head in front of the mirror, remembering that a frown is just a smile turned upside down!

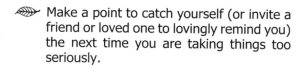 If it helps, tomorrow when you are making breakfast, remember that a boiled egg in the morning is really hard to beat. Come on . . . laugh! Feels good, doesn't it?

56   FEED THE DOG

It isn't that they can't see the solution, it is that they can't see the problem.

~Gilbert K. Chesterton

Once a troubled youth went to his tribal elder and said, "I keep having a very bad dream. In my dreams, there is always a white dog and a black dog fighting each other. I sense that the white dog is good and the black dog is evil, and I am troubled because I don't know which one will win." The elder replied, "The white one will win." The youth replied, "How do you know that is so?" The elder simply smiled and said, "Because that is the dog you will feed."

This well-known story is a metaphor and a classic example of how our minds work for many of us. We spend so much time feeding our minds with conflicting thoughts based on the appearance of evil or negative conditions that it is no wonder the life we live seems like a bad dream at times. My question for you is, Which dog are you feeding today? There are countless opportunities throughout the day to find negative things on which to focus our attention. If we are not mindful, this habit can sweep us right into the collective unconscious, which is where the big black dog of fear has a feeding frenzy. In his great book *The Power of Now*, Eckhart Tolle writes, "Compulsive thinking has become a collective disease. Your whole sense of who you are is derived from mind activity. Your identity, as it is no longer rooted in being, becomes a vulnerable and ever-needy mental construct, which creates fear as the predominant underlying emotion. To become conscious of being, you need to reclaim consciousness from the mind."

The point is this: What we continually focus our energy and attention on becomes that with which we ultimately identify as the basis of our reality! Begin to explore where your mind is taking you. With what are you identifying as the core of your reality? To what are you giving your attention? Either you are rooted in being (God's presence, here and now) or you are rooted in the external world where the mind runs rampant, feeding on the latest fear presented by the media and unconscious others. You can't have it both ways. A house divided always falls. Take a scan of your emotional and physical body as well as the body of your relationships. Is there an unshakable peace present there? Is there a sense of balance and wholeness present there? If you are truly rooted in being, the answer will be a resounding "yes." If your answer is "no," it is safe to assume you are probably feeding the wrong dog. Well, it is never too late to teach an old dog new tricks. Today, you can reclaim consciousness from the mind. You can feed the white dog well!

Mindfulness Practice

- Carry a pen and paper with you today and monitor your thinking: what you read, listen to, watch, and where your conversations with others take you.

- Become a conscious observer of your mind. Set two minutes aside every hour of the day to write down the direction in which your mind is going. This may require a bit of discipline because avoiding this exercise is exactly what the egoic mind (the black dog) wants.

- The first step in being rooted in being is becoming aware of when you are not rooted in being and then making a conscious choice to align with presence in that holy instant.

- At the end of the day, review your notes and, if needed, commit to feeding the white dog a feast tomorrow.

57 SEEK THE SACRED IN THE ORDINARY

The great lesson from the true mystics, from the
Zen monks, and now also from the Humanistic and
Transpersonal psychologists, is that the sacred is in
the ordinary, that it is to be found in one's daily
life . . . in one's own back yard.

~Abraham Maslow

As a facilitator of personal growth, spirituality, and conscious–living workshops for more than twenty years, I have had the honor to share sacred space with countless men and women as they began their journey seeking transformation. What I have discovered is that generally most people begin their spiritual quest because they believe their ordinary lives are not as meaningful, whole, or complete as they could or should be. So, they set out and are very dedicated in their quest, preparing for the big day when they will arrive at that point where their daily life is an extraordinary spiritual experience, full of meaning, whole and complete in every way. If they stick with it, what they discover somewhere along the way is that spirituality and wholeness isn't an extraordinary destination at which they will one day arrive. It's a state of being, which is an ordinary current moment experience.

Too often, we spend our valuable resources and time preparing for the big game only to discover that there is no big game. Life itself is the big game. We cannot sit on the sidelines of life, preparing for it any more than we can one day hope to be more spiritual than we are right now. Spiritually speaking, this is as good as it gets because we are already 100% spirit. Spirituality is simply the practice of being consciously aware of our spiritual nature and the fact that life itself (all of it) is a sacred spiritual experience, including the peaks as well as the valleys, the sunny days and the rainy days, the happy days and the sad days, the healthy days and the sick days. Some of my most rewarding spiritual experiences have happened while sitting in bumper-to-bumper traffic on the freeway, while standing in line at the bank or post office, or even while washing the dishes. There is no less God in any of these places than in my meditation garden or Grace Cathedral for that matter. Our everyday ordinary life is a sacred journey, irrespective of where we are, who we are with, or what we are doing. So we can stop our waiting and looking for God to show up when things are just right . . . because God is already there.

The great Indian poet and mystic Rabindranath Tagore summarized it so beautifully when he wrote, "I have spent my days stringing and unstringing my instrument while the song I came to sing remains unsung." Today is your song—stop rehearsing and sing!

Mindfulness Practice

- Make a conscious decision to enter into this day with an awareness that everything you see, say, think, or do is spiritual in nature.

- Look for God's presence in the ordinary things. If it is a cloudy or stormy day, can you see the beauty and power of God there?

- While waiting in line or at a red light, focus on your breathing and sense the life force within that sustains you so effortlessly.

- Realize that you don't have to be a mystic or even wait for Sunday to have a spiritual experience . . . you are a spiritual experience. Be in awe of it and be thankful for the awareness that it is so.

58   EXCEPT YE BECOME AS LITTLE CHILDREN

*Except ye become as little children, except you can
wake on your fiftieth birthday with the same
forward-looking excitement and interest in life that
you enjoyed when you were five, "ye cannot enter
the kingdom of God." One must not only die daily,
but every day we must be born again.*

~Dorothy L. Sayers

Recently, I flew to Las Vegas to conduct a seminar. As the airplane approached its final destination, the pilot announced apologetically that there would be a slight delay before setting down because high desert winds had forced the airport to close all but one runway. He said that we would be circling the city for a few minutes waiting our turn to land and that we should remain in our seats with our seatbelts securely fastened because there may be a few bumps. Well, that few minutes turned into about forty-five minutes, including a ride that would make the roller–coaster at Six Flags Magic Mountain pale by comparison. The movement was so violent and intense that several passengers actually tossed their cookies, which is a really pleasant way of saying that they fully utilized their personal airsickness bags. As you might guess, that's not generally a good thing to have happen in close quarters because it only served to intensify the discomfort of the situation.

About twenty minutes into the adventure, the entire airplane became very quiet. There was a sense of anxiety and fear that was now palpable while every passenger simply held on for dear life . . . except one. An infant being held in his mother's arms was having a ball! With each dip and bounce of the airplane, he would let out a loud giggle of delight. As I observed this phenomenon, I thought to myself, What is it that he knows and I don't? Then I got it: It wasn't what he knew, it was what he didn't know. He didn't know he supposed to be afraid and concerned for his safety. He didn't know that the odor and stench in the plane was foul. Those were the labels we adults had stuck onto the experience. At that moment, I remembered the passage in the scriptures, "Except ye become as little children . . . " Wow, I thought, now I get it: The mind of this child only knows how to be in the moment. His mind is not wrapped around the past nor projected even five minutes into the future. He is enjoying the ride because he has not yet been taught to fear it. The awareness I received from this child was that the majority of our fears are learned. With that awareness, I took a deep breath and settled back into my seat, pretending I really was on a roller–coaster. I smiled for the rest of the flight. As a matter of fact, I even managed to giggle once or twice, much to the chagrin of the guy sitting next to me holding the barf bag.

How about you? What awareness can you gain from the pure innocence of a child today? The Kingdom of God, which is that place within us where pure peace and unconditional love dwells, can never be entered through the adult mind. That mind is generally so dominated by fear and a need to control, it can't find its way to the door. This is why the great teacher admonished us to become as little children. Note that he didn't say be childish but rather childlike. Take a look at your life and see if maybe it's time for that child within to come out and play. When he or she does, you'll discover that heaven really is at hand . . . and you'll enjoy the ride a lot more.

Mindfulness
Practice

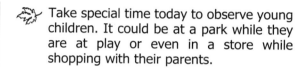 Take special time today to observe young children. It could be at a park while they are at play or even in a store while shopping with their parents.

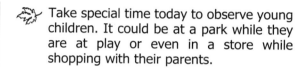 Notice the level of spontaneity, joy, and honesty that flows through children. Notice that they never hold back in the fullness of their expression of life in the moment.

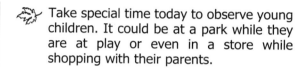 Ask yourself: How can this child be my master teacher today? Be still, listen, and you will know. May this be the day that your child within is truly born again.

59 WEEDING THE GARDEN OF OUR MIND

So plastic is mind, so receptive, that the slightest
thought makes an impression upon it. People who
think many kinds of thought must expect to receive
a confused manifestation in their lives. If a gardener
plants a thousand kinds of seeds, he will get a
thousand kinds of plants; it is the same in mind.

~Dr. Ernest Holmes

One morning, I stepped out onto our second–story balcony and noticed one of our herbal flower boxes had become host to one of the largest weeds I have ever seen (in captivity). We are talking a major league weed here . . . as large as a rosebush. I probably could have pruned it and kept it as my prize plant. So large was this weed that it had taken over the entire box, choking out the fragile herbs recently planted by my wife. I thought to myself, How on earth could a weed like this become rooted in a second–story flower box . . . and then grow to this proportion? The answer to how it got there is simple: either the seed of the weed somehow became commingled with the herbal seeds, a bird dropped it, or perhaps the wind simply blew it into the flower box. Regardless of how it got there, it is no longer there. I lovingly transplanted it into the recycle bin, where in short order its offspring shall find residence in a landfill somewhere. How it grew as large as a Volkswagen before it was discovered and removed is simple too: No one had tended to the flower box for several weeks. Potting soil is incredibly receptive to any seeds introduced to it. It has absolutely no discretion when it comes to playing host to seeds; it says "yes" to all of them. The point: An unattended flower box in March can mean unseen havoc for your daffodils.

So it is too with your mind: An unattended mind can create havoc for you because your mind is amazingly receptive to whatever suggestions may be dropped into it. It has been said that the subconscious mind cannot take a joke. This simply means that whatever is introduced to it, it takes as serious instruction to grow that thought-seed into a full-blown plant—be it a rose or a weed, it doesn't care. Just like that receptive potting soil in my flower box, the subconscious mind says "yes" to all seeds planted, positive or otherwise. When you stop and consider how many thought-seeds are blown, dropped, or purposefully planted in your mind on a daily basis, it may cause you to tend to your mental garden with a bit more regularity. In addition to all the seeds that were planted in your mind before you knew you even had one, your mind hears the radio, the TV, or even others talking in a restaurant irrespective of whether you are conscious of it or not. When you engage in gossip or negative conversation with or about others, your subconscious mind hears it all. Here is the hook: It takes it personally . . . about you. The only way to avoid this type of mind pollution is to be consciously focused on what you want to have planted and growing in your flower box called life. We are talking 24/7 here.

The action you and I need to take is clear, isn't it? It is proven that the human mind thinks thousands of thoughts a day. Instead of planting a mixed bag of thousands of various seeds (confused and unfocused thinking) that will require a full-time gardener to pull up the weeds, specialize in planting one or two types of seed. Plant thought-seeds about yourself and others that are rooted in reverence and loving-kindness. Plant seeds that focus on God's presence at the center and circumference of all you say, think, and do at work, home, or play. Be mindful. Be skillful in the seeds you plant and how you nurture them. Your life is your garden; keep the weeds out because that is one way in which you can personally beautify our world. You owe that much to yourself and to those who receive the benefit of the seeds you drop along the way.

Mindfulness
Practice

➣ Keep a journal for the next twenty-four hours.

➣ Make note of all the different thought-seeds that become obvious to you throughout the day. By this, I mean repetitive or habitual thoughts, either positive or negative. Don't judge what you find, simply write them down.

➣ At the end of the day, sit quietly and review your findings. If you discover thought-seeds that are growing beautiful experiences for you, see yourself planting even more of those seeds.

➣ If you notice any pattern of thinking from which "weeds" will grow or are currently growing, simply visualize yourself plucking the thought-weed from your mind and immediately plant a thought-seed that supports the idea of wholeness. Follow it with an affirmation such as "Divine mind knows how to grow a beautiful life by means of me, and I am grateful it is so."

➣ You may have to do this any number of times, but it is your garden . . . and you are the only gardener who can tend to it.

60

THE SACRED
INCLUDES YOU!

*If you love the sacred and despise the ordinary, you
are still bobbing in the ocean of delusion.*

~Lin-Chi

Recently, I spent time at a spiritual retreat at the Asilomar
Conference Center in Pacific Grove, California, which is located
at the very tip of the Monterey Peninsula. It is without question one the
most breathtaking spots to which I have ever been. In the past
twenty-seven years, I have spent many weeks (or more) there,
communing with my peers and with nature. Asilomar is one of those
places that seems to have a sense of sacredness to it. With the ocean, the
wildlife, and the amazing trees, it is not too difficult to actually feel the
presence of God oozing through all of it. Even the people on retreat
seem to ooze God essence. Just prior to leaving, as I stood on the back
deck of the very room in which I had stayed perhaps twenty years ago
and looked at the beauty that lay before me, I found myself saying,
"This place is timeless . . . .It is as beautiful and sacred as it was the
first time I set foot on these grounds in 1977 . . . .Nothing has
changed." At that moment, a voice, which over the years has become
known to me as divine love, spoke gently to me, and It said, "Oh yes,
something has changed. You, my beloved, have changed." With that
simple revelation, I began to weep. It was true: The Asilomar grounds
were as sacred as they always have been, but I had changed. I too had
become sacred. Not that I could ever be more or less sacred in God's
eyes but in my own.

The truth is, life is a sacred experience for all of us; it always has
been and always shall be. We cannot become more spiritual than we
are in this holy instant—we are already 100% spirit. It's about

awakening to this truth. That's what makes you and me sacred. That's what the practice of spirituality does; it awakens us to who we have always been. We don't have to go to a retreat center to know this. Granted, it may be easier to learn about and remember our spiritual connectedness to God while in an Asilomar setting, but the opportunity to really practice it comes when we get home from "camp consciousness." Our human tendency is to label some places, some people, and some events as more sacred or spiritual than others. In 1977, that was how I saw life: through the eyes of duality. I saw Asilomar as a sacred place, and I went there in search of a spiritual experience, never realizing I already was a spiritual experience. The reality is, our everyday ordinary lives can be transformed into a spiritual experience simply by remembering to remember that there can be no more of God at a spiritual retreat than on the 405 freeway at 6:00 p.m. (I bet you have never thought of a concrete freeway as sacred ground, have you?) As my friend Walter Starcke says, "It's all God . . . so love it all." Your entire life is a sacred experience, so you can go through life looking for an experience, "out there" or you can awaken to the fact that you are a spiritual experience, wherever you are and whatever you're doing. Don't wait until your next spiritual retreat to know that this is so. Know that you are loved and supported today on your quest to awaken to your own divine splendor in every holy instant.

Mindfulness Practice

🍃 Choose a place where you have no trouble experiencing a strong sense of God's presence, perhaps a garden, church sanctuary, or park. Spend time in that place deepening your experience of the divine and feel it permeate the essence of your being.

🍃 Then, the next time you are in a place that you may have labeled as less than spiritual (e.g., the workplace, the post office, the gym) pause, take a conscious deep breath, and remember the feeling you had when you had the strong sense of God's presence.

🍃 Stay with that feeling until you realize that in that holy instant you are standing on sacred ground. You are not just having a spiritual experience, you are the personification of God's presence. You are a spiritual experience. The sacred includes you.

61   GOOD THINGS CAN GROW IN THE DARK

All growth is a leap in the dark, a spontaneous,
unpremeditated act without benefit of experience.

~Henry Miller

As I opened the door and stepped into the darkness of my kitchen pantry to grab my box of Cheerios this morning, I looked down and noticed a bag of potatoes, which had been sitting on the floor for a few weeks. Upon closer examination, I could see that most of the potatoes had begun to push out little sprouts. As any potato aficionado knows, the sprouts are an indication that the potato is trying to grow—and even the darkness of a pantry can't stop it from doing so. It is well documented that if one wants to see the spud sprout rapidly, all one needs to do is place the potato in the light of day. Keeping them in the dark slows down the process, but even in total darkness, there is something within the potato that knows it's supposed to seek growth and expansion, despite its poor growing conditions.

Therein lies the lesson: As strange as this may sound, you and I have a great deal in common with the potato. That same "something" lies within each of us and is constantly seeking growth and expansion through us. Even our darkest of times can't stop it from having its way. The primary difference is that the potato has no choice in the matter, whereas it appears that we think we do. For our purposes here, the darkness can symbolize challenging times, or it can simply represent the unknown. Often, we seek "perfect" growing conditions before we sprout new life. We prefer the comfort of being able to see where we are growing. Wouldn't it be great if all of our growth opportunities came in times of light, love, blue skies, and green lights, where it felt good and we could see where we are going?

Unfortunately, that's not the way it works. The reality is, we are destined to grow, one way or another. Our only choice is, Will it be consciously or unconsciously? There can be great personal growth for us as we learn to consciously push out into the darkness as well as the light. The truth is that some of our most meaningful personal growth experiences can be stimulated when life appears the darkest and most uncertain. The darkness doesn't seem to stifle the growth of a potato, and you know where mushrooms grow—buried deeply in a pile of manure! Perhaps nature's wisdom has much to teach us about growth.

Is it time for you to sprout some new growth? If the answer is "yes," don't wait until "growing conditions" are perfect, because they seldom are. Don't turn away from your dark or uncertain times, lean into them and invite the wisdom of the infinite present there to reveal the meaning and purpose of the moment. Let the experience become your teacher. Push out into life and grow, regardless of the conditions, because that's why you are here—to evolve and grow into the spectacular being you are!

Mindfulness Practice

- Let this be the day that you allow your challenge, setback, or uncertainty to become your stimulus for conscious and personal growth. As you take time to look directly into the face of that challenge, setback, or uncertainty, invite the inherent wisdom of God moving in, through, and as you to reveal what you need to know in order to grow consciously.

- Personalize the experience and welcome those times by trusting and knowing that there is as much of God's presence in a kitchen pantry as there is in the Sistine Chapel.

62

Life is short, but there is always time for courtesy.

~Ralph Waldo Emerson

Most of us would agree that we are living in a world where much of what we do somehow incorporates the use of computers and, more specifically, cell phones. With the advancement of this technology, time seems to be getting more and more compressed. What I have observed is that in this state of compression, many people are becoming less and less considerate of others.

I had a rather startling demonstration of that one Sunday morning as I was presenting our opening prayer meditation during our 10:00 a.m. service. Several minutes into the meditation, the lights had been dimmed and there was a beautiful stillness washing over everyone in the sanctuary. People were settling deeply into the quiet dignity of sacred communion with God . . . that is, until someone's cell phone rang and rang and rang. It was a lovely, catchy little tune, but it nonetheless proved to be more than a bit distracting for most of those present. I paused for a brief moment to refocus my attention, thinking not thoughts of anger toward the individual whose phone was ringing but thoughts of sadness that this person might be so attached to the world that he or she couldn't give themselves (and others) the gift of one hour of quality time for spiritual communion. I understand there are always exceptions to the rule, such as a physician who may be on call, but that's why God created pagers that vibrate.

Daily, we observe the same thing happening in restaurants, theaters, grocery stores, public bathrooms, and most certainly, automobiles on the highway. I wonder how we ever survived before the invention of the cell phone! Of course, we did survive for centuries without that electronic gizmo attached to our ear, and we could now as well, couldn't we? Let's get real here: Our need (addiction) to stay connected to the world 24/7 may be getting in the way of being authentically connected to God and fully engaged in life in the moment, wherever we may be.

I know this is a delicate issue because any one of us could probably find ourselves somewhere in the description of the people above who use cell phones in a manner that perhaps encroaches on other people's space not to mention their safety. Rather than intrude on our own and other people's sacred space, we could be practicing mindfulness and spirituality by being fully present wherever we are. If we want to ponder how many of us tend to abuse the use of cell phones from an even more basic and logical perspective, I invite you to consider the essence of Emerson's statement in today's quote: While life is indeed short or compressed, it's no excuse to be less than courteous to our fellow human beings.

The question is, Can we find enough time to stay connected to the world in a manner that also honors and respects others? Of course we can . . . when we set our intention to do so. The spiritual reality is that whether in a sanctuary on Sunday morning or on a busy freeway at 5:00 p.m. on Friday night, God is there, and wherever God is there is a divine continuum of time—we just need to become aware of it. Time is all we really have, so enjoy it and also support others in doing the same. Showing them courtesy in a manner that also allows them to enjoy the moment at hand is how we do it. When you really stop and think about it, there's always enough time to be courteous, yes? So, stop . . . and really think about it. It's your call!

Mindfulness
Practice

🍂 Just for today, try to live without using your cell phone while in the presence of others.

🍂 If you need to conduct business on a cell phone, do so with a mindfulness of the impact it has on others around you.

🍂 If you can get by without using a cell phone for one full day, observe how that makes you feel. Use that time to make a connection of a different kind—call on your awareness of the presence of God wherever you are and have a conversation . . . but listen more than you talk.

63

AS WITHIN, SO WITHOUT

Our life is shaped by our mind; we become what we think. Suffering follows an evil thought as the wheels of a cart follow the oxen that draw it . . . joy follows a pure thought like a shadow that never leaves.

~The Dhammapada

Have you ever seen a sculptor work with stone? That raw hunk of rock is nothing but rock until he decides what it is he wants to create. It is but a formless mass of unrealized potential until he realizes his vision, picks up the carving tools, and goes to work. Then the rock begins to take on the form and character that manifests the inner blueprint. The sculptor simply removes the unnecessary pieces of rock and presto! that which began with the energy of a thought becomes transformed.

Now, begin to see yourself as a master sculptor. Each thought you have is another chip in your unrealized potential, your future, your life. Understanding that your mind (where your beliefs are formed) is the point of origin for every thought you have, it is encouraging to know that it is not the accidental slip of your carving tool that does the real damage. By this I mean that an occasional negative thought related to fear, judgment, jealousy, or _____ (fill in the blank) will not ruin your creation. However, the same thought repeated over and over countless times is bound to put quite an indentation in the stone. This will weaken the foundation upon which a healthy life is built. Throughout time, every spiritual master from every age and teaching has taught this same truth. It is a reality from which we cannot escape: As a man thinketh, so he is. It is done unto you as you believe.

Buddha was right. Our lives are shaped by our minds. We really do become what we think. The good news is that it is never too late to begin carving out a new concept of ourselves if we don't care for the shape our life is taking. It starts with your next thought. So, sharpen your tools and go for it.

Mindfulness Practice

➣ What are you thinking? As a rule of thumb, what is the direction, tone, and intent of your predominate thoughts? Ask yourself, "What kind of life is my mind shaping for me?" Awareness of your thoughts is where it begins.

➣ Monitor the thoughts you think today. See how they have shaped your life up until now and how they will form your destiny.

➣ If you catch yourself chipping away at the foundation of your own happiness and joy, stop and invite the indwelling presence of God to help you craft a new thought.

➣ Yes, it is that easy—and that hard! You may have to do it a thousand times a day, but you are worth the effort, yes?

64

THROUGH THE
EYES OF GOD

Spirituality is natural goodness. God is not a person; God is a Presence personified in us. Spirituality is not a thing; it is the atmosphere of God's Presence, goodness, truth and beauty.

~Dr. Ernest Holmes

A mother views her child
Through the eyes of love
A scientist views the stars
In the heavens above
A doctor views his patient
With compassion and concern
A student views his teacher
With so much to learn
A grandma views her grandchild
And makes such a fuss
While God views Itself
Through the eyes of each of us.

How do you view your life today? Most of us are so deeply rooted in the world of work, people, conditions, places, and things that we seldom think of taking time to step back and see our lives through the eyes of God. When we do, it is easy to remember that God is all there is and that we are the living embodiment of the divine. This remembrance tends to encourage us to walk, talk, and act with a greater sense of reverence. In that realization, every moment, every thing, and every one becomes sacred. Practicing the presence of God is the practice of spirituality. It's that simple—and that hard. How is your practice going?

Mindfulness Practice	ᔓ Remembering that God is all there is, imagine what God must be experiencing through you every time you enter into that sacred space of being aware that you are one with It.
	ᔓ Now go look in a mirror and realize that this is God looking at Itself. Amazing realization, isn't it?

65

ARE YOU SEEKING
A SPIRITUAL LIFE,
OR IS IT SEEKING
YOU?

*Many of us incorrectly assume that a spiritual life
begins when we change what we normally do in our
daily life. We feel we must change our job, our
living situation, our relationship, our address, our
diet, or our clothes before we can truly begin a
spiritual practice. And yet it is not the act but the
awareness, the vitality, and the kindness we bring
to our work that allows it to become sacred.*

~Wayne Muller

Once in a while, I will have a first–time visitor at our center seek me
out after the Sunday Celebration Service just to tell me that they
have finally found the spiritual home they have been seeking for so
long. They have finally had the spiritual experience they just couldn't
get at "all the other churches" they have visited, and I will absolutely,
unquestionably, without a doubt see them again next week so that they
can continue to deepen their spiritual life! Seldom do I see them in the
following weeks or any time thereafter. Why? Because the spiritual
glow wore off twenty minutes after they left the parking lot, and they
are off at some other church, continuing their quest. Human nature is
funny, isn't it? Many of those most desperate for a spiritual life
continue to look for it outside of themselves, believing that it has to
come through some sacred entity or that it can simply be scheduled for
a Sunday morning between 9:00 and 10:30 a.m. The truth is, while
some religions and ministers would love to have us believe it, the
church isn't responsible or, for that matter, capable of giving anyone a

spiritual experience or lifestyle. A church, a minister, and rituals are great reminders of our connectedness to God, but the experience must always be "an inside job." As for a lifestyle, what about the other six and a half days of the week? This is where mindfulness comes in.

The fact is, life is a spiritual experience—we simply need to awaken to it. In the Zen tradition, there is a statement that speaks to this beautifully: "Before enlightenment, chop wood and carry water. After enlightenment, chop wood and carry water." There is as much of God's presence in us and around us when we are mowing the lawn, taking a shower, taking out the trash, signing a business deal, or changing the baby's diaper as there is in the most sacred temple, ashram, mosque, or church on the planet. We don't have to change into any special clothes or even say any special words. It's as simple as remembering to remember that every action we take is sacred . . . every relationship we enter into in the course of the day is sacred . . . every breath is sacred . . . every holy instant is sacred . . . your life is a sacred thing. Why? Because God is all that is. This simple remembrance will change how we see our world and how we interact with it. Remembering to remember that God is all that is will transform everything you say, think, and do into a sacred act. All of a sudden, the awareness is that you are not just having a spiritual experience, a spiritual experience is actually having you. That is a profound thought, isn't it? Think about this: You don't have to seek a spiritual experience, you are a spiritual experience. You don't have to seek a spiritual experience because a spiritual experience is seeking you—that is simply God seeking expression in, through, and as you. Now all you need to do is be aware of it.

Mindfulness Practice

- Make a conscious decision to live your life in micromoments today.

- Be aware of the divine intelligence that animates and sustains your body.

- For today, when you shower and every time you wash your hands, marvel at how the soap and water feel as you rub your hands together and over your body. Become aware of how the muscles in your hands move your fingers to grip the soap, making the job seem effortless. Just imagine the intelligence it takes to get your body to do this simple task without you telling it how!

- Then realize that you've just had a spiritual experience.

- Now see where else you can expand this mindfulness practice.

66   WHEREVER YOU GO, THERE YOU ARE

Self-acceptance comes from meeting life's challenges vigorously. Don't numb yourself to your trials and difficulties, nor build mental walls to exclude pain from your life. You will find peace not by trying to escape your problems, but by confronting them courageously. You will find peace not in denial, but in victory.

~J. Donald Walters

Often, the most powerful and meaningful lessons in life come gift-wrapped in pain. When I say pain, I mean emotional as well as physical pain. In general, I believe that our culture is more accepting of physical pain than we are of emotional pain. Just about everyone in physical pain will sooner or later seek out the help of a physician. Our culture has made it acceptable to be in physical pain. However, when it comes to emotional pain, there seems to be great resistance to seeking professional help as if it is shameful to be hurting emotionally. What I have discovered in counseling people who are in deep emotional pain is that there is a desire to deny or avoid it rather than deal with the issues that cause the pain. The tendency is to numb the pain through drugs (legal and illegal), alcohol or some other substance of choice, overindulgence in food or sex, or even radical adrenalin-rush activities—anything that will take one's mind off the pain. In some extreme cases, I have talked with people who have considered suicide as a way to end the pain. The best counsel I can offer to anyone who may fit into one or more of the aforementioned categories can be found in the title of one of my favorite books by author Jon Kabat-Zinn, *Wherever You Go, There You Are*. The following bit of wisdom is profoundly true, so I urge you to consider it carefully. Irrespective of what "trip" you take to avoid your emotional pain, upon your return, it will always be waiting for you like a loyal pet. That even extends to the ultimate avoidance action, suicide. How can this be? Who you really are does not end with the demise of your physical body. Your soul self continues on its journey of unfoldment, taking with it all of your unresolved issues. My point: You have eternity to get it right but why put it off? The interesting thing is that whether in this life or the next, the people and circumstances that cause you emotional pain are only stimuli to activate that place within you that is in need of healing. Wherever you go, you will manifest the people and circumstances that, over and over again, offer you a chance to heal the pain. There is no better place than here, no better time than now, to find the peace you may be missing out on.

Mindfulness Practice

First, you must turn and face your demons. You will discover that as you drag your emotional pain into the light of day and look at it fearlessly, it's not nearly as big as you thought it was in the darkness of your mind.

If you need help in doing this, seek out the support of a minister, therapist, or good and trusted friend . . . and go for it.

Know you never stand alone, because the infinite power of God (the ultimate light) dwells within you. Step into the presence of that light with a clear mind and an open heart, and you will find victory in the eternal moment of now.

With God, all things are possible. Believe it.

67

*Every thought you have travels through your
biological system and activates a physiological
response. Some thoughts — like fear, are like depth
charges, causing a reaction throughout your body; a
loving thought can relax your entire body. Some
thoughts are more subtle, and still others are
unconscious.*

~Carolyn Myss

Recently, while reading a book written by Vietnamese Buddhist
master Thich Nhat Hahn, a statement he made regarding the
movies and TV programs we watch caught my attention. When I read
the statement quoted above by Carolyn Myss, it all clicked and I
understood the importance of being mindful of the source of the
thought energy we allow to move through us. Thich Nhat Hahn wrote,
"Movies are food for our eyes, ears and minds. When we watch TV, the
program is our food . . . when you feel despair, fear, or depression, it
may be because you have ingested too many toxins through your sense
impressions. Not only children need to be protected from violent and
unwholesome films, TV programs, books, magazines and games. We,
too, can be destroyed by the media."

When we couple that statement with Carolyn Myss's quote, it
becomes more obvious why so many people's lives seem to be in such
a state of disrepair. The fact is that there are some wonderful movies
and TV programs available to us today, and there are some
not-so-wonderful movies and TV programs available to us today. I
wonder, if people understood more fully the impact that their
thoughts had on their bodies and the body of their affairs, would
they be more mindful of the "food" they consume with their minds?

Simply put, thoughts energized by fear, violence, and negative images move energy through us in a manner that causes great dis-ease, emotionally and physically, whereas thoughts energized by love moves energy in a manner that manifests as relaxation and inner peace. In my opinion, this is a no-brainer—I don't have to think twice about this one. How about you?

How are you choosing your mind's food? Too often, we operate on autopilot, settling for anything that will distract the mind from a stressful day, emotional or physical pain, or even boredom for that matter. I invite you to join me today in being attentively aware of what you are feeding your mind. Isn't conscious living great?

Mindfulness Practice

- Understanding that your thoughts are only the offspring of your beliefs, be willing to challenge what you believe when you become aware of what you are feeding your mind today.

- If you catch yourself "feeding" on programming that perpetuates fear, violence, cruelty, or disrespect, be willing to ask yourself, "What's going on in my belief system that would cause me to want to feed myself this toxic meal of negative energy?"

- And then listen. It's amazing how available infinite intelligence is and how willing it is to lead you to higher ground when you ask for guidance.

- If led to do so, you just have to muster up the willingness to turn the channel or select a movie that you know will feed your mind a meal that serves your wholeness. So eat well, because you are worth it!

68

GETTING OUT OF THE PROBLEM AND INTO THE SOLUTION

Whatever we identify ourselves with we tend to become. Whatever we think about gradually becomes a subconscious pattern, always tending to manifest itself in our experience.

~Dr. Ernest Holmes

Do this visualization with me: Imagine an incredibly huge lake. It is clean and full of crystal clear water from which all humankind draws to fill its needs. Now visualize a single pipeline draining into the lake from a nearby factory. From this factory and into the lake flows all the factory's toxic waste. At this point, there is only one factory so the lake doesn't show many signs of pollution. Now imagine that daily, hundreds of new factories are built, with each factory spewing its toxic waste into the same lake. Finally, tens of millions of factories are all doing the same thing. Soon the lake is full of poison, which contaminates all the people who use it.

The lake symbolizes the collective unconscious of humankind. In metaphysics, it is referred to as "race mind," because it is the point in the unseen collective mind where the entire human race dumps its beliefs and thoughts, be they positive and loving or fearful, hateful, and toxic. My point is simple. The more people focusing on the negative, pouring forth fear, worry, resentment, and hate, the more toxins flow into the lake of humankind's collective consciousness, and it poisons us all. This isn't just about Americans but includes every person on the planet who thinks a thought that is backed by a strong negative feeling! It all goes into that lake. This lesson is a vital reminder for me too. Like most Americans, I sat with my eyes glued to the television on September 11, 2001, watching in slow motion replay after replay of the incredible tragedy and horror to which our brothers and sisters in New York and Washington, D.C., were subjected. In addition, I spent countless hours discussing it with many others, replaying it all again in my mind. However, the above comment from Dr. Ernest Holmes makes it very clear that to remain focused on any problem simply exacerbates it. When we multiply our individual energy, which we pour into that race mind, times many millions of people, we are adding something very powerful to the collective unconscious. We simply have to ask ourselves, What good comes from continuing to focus our energies on the problem?

Of course, the media do their best to keep the country informed of our nation's tragedies, but at some point, the media turn into the same misuse of human emotionalism they have preyed on for years. Tragedy and fear sells! If we want to clean up our collective "lake," at some point, we have to stop buying. This is definitely not to say we discount, deny, or ignore this tragedy and assault on all humanity—just the opposite. It means that at some point, we must, as they say in recovery programs, "get out of the problem and into the solution." The solution isn't just eradicating terrorism from the face of the planet, it is changing the content of what we are all pouring into the collective unconscious. It is time to clean up the lake! For those of us who want to begin living in the solution, it can start with making sure that our daily contribution of thoughts and feelings that flow into the collective unconscious are purified and nontoxic. Moving away from the gravitational pull of the race mind is not easy because it is very strong, but it can be done. It starts with your very next thought. What will it be?

Mindfulness Practice

- Visualize a pipeline leading directly from your mind into the "lake" of the collective unconscious.

- Begin to focus on the presence of God moving through you into the lake. Remember that God is love in Its highest vibration. See love flowing into that lake, purifying and cleaning it.

- Now visualize hundreds of millions of human beings around this world doing the same thing. Today, think thoughts that come from wholeness and love. That is the greatest contribution to the healing of this planet you could make.

69   YOU ARE GOD'S SEEDLING

The seed of God is in us. Given an intelligent and hard-working farmer, it will thrive and grow up to God, whose seed it is; and accordingly its fruits will be God-nature. Pear seeds grow into pear trees, nut seeds into nut trees, and God-seed into God.

~Meister Eckhart

Several weeks ago, while facilitating a mindfulness retreat at a beautiful farm near our center, I had an "aha" experience I would like to share with you. My personal focus for the day was on deepening my understanding of what the next step on my spiritual path is supposed to be and how that related to my purpose in life. With all the fear and confusion that is going on around our planet, it was as if I had temporarily lost touch with any awareness of my spiritual connection with life and was struggling to regain it. Yes, there are days when we all need to "remember to remember" who we are and why we are here. This particular day while walking a labyrinth that had been set up in the middle of a magnificent walnut grove, I noticed what appeared to be little green limes on the ground, such as you might expect to find falling from a lime tree. But in a walnut grove? I picked up several of them and brought them home to observe. Over the next two weeks, the soft green husks shriveled up and walnuts clearly emerged! I still have them as a reminder that all things in life begin as seedlings, and there is an intelligence within the seed that knows what it is supposed to be, even when the outer world may hold different opinions. What strikes me most is that even a walnut (as all living things do) has a calling. It never doubts what it was created to be. It simply (and literally) "lets go and lets God," trusting that the divine intelligence within it knows how to evolve into what it is naturally.

In much the same way, I believe that you and I are God's seedlings, each with a calling perhaps yet unrealized. As Meister Eckhart stated, "The seed of God is in us," so there must also lie within us a calling or purpose that sleeps until the proper growing season calls it into fruition. It knows what we came to be, even if we are uncertain at this moment. Great inner peace can be a reality for each of us when we remember to remember that. Not only does God know what we are supposed to be but God also knows how to grow us into that which we are supposed to be. My point: If the seed of God is an inherent part of who we are, in those times of doubt we can stop trying so hard to have a spiritual experience and realize we are a spiritual experience. It doesn't matter what season of our growth we are in, there is no less God present in the seed than in the tree. Our job is to grow into an awareness and an acceptance that it is so today, even if we appear to be "green" to the rest of the world. If pear seeds grow into pear trees and walnut seeds grow into walnut trees, you and I are truly destined to grow into the full expression of the divine. Let your roots sink into that!

Mindfulness Practice

- Take a walk through an area that has mature trees that are dropping seeds or fruit. Find a seed (within the fruit if necessary) and hold it in your hand and then close your eyes. Imagine that you are holding a fully grown tree in your hand, complete and whole in every way, because in reality you are. Everything that is needed for that seed to grow into a tree is inherent within that seed.

- Be in awe of that incredible truth and dwell on the fact that the same thing can be said about you. The wholeness that God is resides within you. Remember that the seed of God is in you—always has been, always will be. You are God's seedling!

70

THE WONDER OF IT ALL

When a load of bricks, dumped on a corner lot, can arrange themselves into a house; when a handful of springs and screws and wheels, emptied on a desk, can gather themselves into a watch, then and not until then will it seem sensible, to some of us at least, to believe that all these thousands or millions of worlds could have been created, balanced and set to revolving in their separate orbits — all without any directing Intelligence at all.

~Bruce Barton

Have you ever spent time allowing your mind to wander and wonder? Have you ever thought about how incredible it is that you can read and decipher these words and draw meaning from them? Have you ever contemplated in amazement how your body works, maintaining itself to a large degree without any help from you? Have you taken time to contemplate what causes your heart to beat and what turned the breakfast you had this morning into skin, fingernails, and hair? Have you ever taken just a few moments to simply stare at a beautiful flower and notice the incredible patterns and colors that not even the greatest artist could recreate? Have you ever looked up at the stars and planets at night and been in awe of the expansiveness of it all, perhaps even wondering if there might be some other being on some distant planet looking back at ours at the same time, wondering the same thing? Have you ever thought about what holds the planets and stars in place? Have you ever gazed into a newborn baby's eyes and seen the infinite presence of pure spirit looking back at you and been in awe of the fact that this being just came from the absolute essence, God? How can you or I do any of these things and not feel like an intricate and significant part of something far greater and grander than the "little me"?

I have done all these things, and I can tell you that in part, it is what keeps me sane, grounded, and spiritually connected to God, life, and purpose when the world seems to be getting more and more crazy each day. This also includes those times when I tend to get too enmeshed in my own personal trauma dramas. Life is always manifesting purpose; all we need to do is think about the miracle of it all. So, the next time you feel as if you are getting caught up in the frenzy of the world or your personal life begins to look like a bad soap opera, take some time and consider some of the above questions. Give yourself the gift of a sacred moment in the now. With great and clear intention, contemplate and connect with the miracle of life, where God is always present. Celebrate your unity with God . . . and truly be in awe. The word awe is the root from which the word "awesome" comes . . . and that is what you really are. Not because I say so but because God is awesome, and what God is, so too are you. It's just a matter of taking time to think about the wonder of it all.

Mindfulness Practice

- Begin your meditation today by doing a mental scan of your physical body. Starting with your feet and working your way up to the top of your head, become aware of the presence of the life force. Is there life in your toes . . . your spleen . . . your heart . . . your spine . . . your brain? Of course, the answer is yes.

- Be in awe of it. Then, as you go out into the world today, carry that awareness with you. Feel that presence throughout the day.

- Extend your awareness of that presence as you are out in nature. Stop and really look into a flower. Watch an animal in its natural environment. Tonight, spend a few minutes out of doors, gazing at the stars and moon.

- Feel the same presence out there as you do within. Before you go to bed, again, take a mental body scan and you will feel that presence stronger than ever.

- Life really is awesome, isn't it?

71

CHOOSE YOUR
OWN WAY

_____

The last of the human freedoms – to choose one's
attitude in any given set of circumstances, to choose
one's own way.

~Victor Frankl

Victor Frankl's confinement in a Nazi prison camp qualifies him by virtue of the experience to make the above statement. He discovered that while others around us may be able to control our immediate environment, including the conditions we encounter, they cannot control our attitude. The ability to control our experience in life takes on a new depth and meaning when we come to the realization that the only thing we really have even a modicum of control over is our own mind. What happens in our mind determines if we shall react or respond to that which is set before us at any given moment.

This is a reality that touches every area of our lives. An attachment to needing to control our every circumstance is a recipe for suffering. As an example, from time to time, as I work with couples for whom I am asked to perform a wedding ceremony, I see major–league disappointment and frustration pending as their wedding day nears. When the bride-to-be pulls out her three-page agenda, outlining exactly the way it is supposed to be down to the minute that they kiss, she is putting her peace, tranquility, and joy in the hands of a number of other people and circumstances that are beyond her control. Invariably, the flowers or the musicians are late, sweet little ring bearers sometimes lose diamond rings in the grass, a bridesmaid (or a groom) passes out, it rains, a baby cries, an airplane does a 100-foot flyby towing a "Drink Budweiser" banner, a bee lands on the best man's head, the bride perspires so badly her makeup runs, and so on.

The illusion (fantasy) is that we have control over much; the reality is we have control over little more than our next thought, which dictates how we will choose to experience the moment and the event at hand. No one can rob us of the freedom to choose what our next thought will be. While we don't always have the ability to change or control other people and events, we can absolutely choose to change our thoughts and perspectives about people and events. In a very powerful way, this puts us in charge of our life experience in every holy instant, irrespective of what it may look like. You will be choosing your own way. That is a powerful place to be in consciousness. Try it and see.

Mindfulness Practice	
	Make a decision today to fine-tune your awareness that while you may not be able to control the behavior of those around you, the weather, or certain events and conditions, you have absolute control over how you choose to experience them.
	You can "alter the altitude of your attitude" in an instant. Awareness is the key.
	Your attachment to that over which you have no control will make you suffer.
	Let go—let God. Now breathe and simply be.

72

GENIUS AND THE
"D" WORD

*You have in your composition a mighty Genius for
expression which has escaped discipline.*

~H. G. Wells

Have you ever wondered why some people seem to demonstrate what appears to be superior intelligence, talents, and creative abilities with such apparent ease and sense of effortlessness? In traditional mental science, such individuals might be referred to as geniuses. The belief is that there are but a select few who are born with genius. In metaphysics, many refer to this as the creative genius, perhaps a karmic endowment brought forward from some prior lifetime. I don't subscribe to either of these theories. I believe that God cannot discriminate when it comes to handing out the gifts of genius. Granted, the gifts may vary from person to person, but no one has ever been left out, because genius is an inherent fundamental essence that lies within every human being, waiting to be revealed and released. It is how God finds fuller expression of Itself by means of us.

So why is it that some people are able to launch their genius, sharing it with the world in productive, purposeful, and expressive ways while others just never seem to get off the launching pad? The gift lies within all human beings. No doubt some individuals may be required to dig a little deeper and for a longer period of time than others to uncover it. Perhaps that is why there is so much frustration in many people's lives. Everyone feels the inner stirring of that creative genius that is seeking fuller expression through him or her. Some people are naturally led to honor the stirring, doing whatever needs to be done to nurture it and call it forward. They sense the creative inner urge as natural and so they flow with it, allowing it to have its way through them. How they express their genius appears easy for them, and it is because they don't resist it. This doesn't mean that they don't work hard at developing the gifts, because they usually do, it just doesn't appear to be hard work because they have surrendered to it. Genius is just the energy of divine intelligence seeking an outlet. The person who is not honoring the stirring of their genius is likely to feel it as misdirected energy flowing through them. It can show up in the form of a short attention span, restlessness, boredom, short–temperedness, and can even result in destructive actions. (Energy has to have an outlet.)

Never doubt for even one minute that there is genius within you, awaiting your recognition of it. No matter what the gift of your genius may be, the magic ingredient in manifesting it is always the same: discipline! The "D" word sends chills down many a spine, and there are times when I resist it with all my might. When I do catch myself resisting the D word, I often use this visualization: Think of discipline as a drilling tool, boring through all the layers of resistance, cutting straight through to the core of your creative genius. See the energy of that genius flowing out into expression through you. Discipline gives focus and direction to our energy of intention, which in turn unleashes the genius. So, the word for the day is discipline. Where in your life is your inner genius waiting for you to call it forward? Invoke the D word and do the work. You will be well pleased with what is revealed.

Mindfulness Practice

➣ Begin to explore any areas in your life where you may feel the energy of frustration, restlessness, or boredom stirring. What could you be doing differently to enhance your experience?

➣ Ask yourself if you are using the discipline you know is required to find greater expression in that area of your life. It begins with intention, clarity, and right effort.

➣ Is your genius stirring, waiting for you to let it out? Where do you begin honoring your genius? To find it, look at what you most resist doing now . . . and do it!

73

SHEDDING THE LIGHT ON ENLIGHTENMENT

Before enlightenment, chop wood and carry water . . . after enlightenment, chop wood and carry water.

~Ancient Buddhist wisdom

Throughout the millennia, enlightenment has been touted as the brass ring on the spiritual path, the highest accomplishment a soul could ever obtain while in Earth school. Personally, I think this whole enlightenment thing is overrated. I mean, think about it: Once you reach enlightenment, what else is there? Life would become boring and meaningless, right? There'd be no more problems: no more attachment to winning conflicts and arguments with family, friends, and even strangers, no more attachment to material gain or loss, no more attachment to people's opinions of you, no more having to go to work at the same old boring job, no more having to exercise and honor our bodies. In other words, all of these daily challenges would simply dissolve into the ethers and be no more, right? WRONG!

Masters from every tradition have said the same thing regarding enlightenment: Nothing changes but one's perception, and with a shift in perception comes a new experience and reality. It has been reported that with enlightenment comes a new way of seeing life. Everything becomes a spiritual experience because all sense of separation melts away, revealing only divine essence. An enlightened being sees nothing less than pure God in, through, and as all. It is as if a divine sublimation has melded all energy into a very present moment experience, irrespective of what one may be doing. In other words, after enlightenment, we still have to go to work, do the dishes, mow the lawn, live with our family and neighbors, and exercise and honor our bodies. We simply do it with a new sense of being connected to the divine flow of life. Do we have to wait for enlightenment before we can live with a sense of connectedness to life where we find peace, balance, and harmony? What is enlightenment really? It is living in a state of conscious awareness that God is all there is. The fact is, every day can be a new day of enlightenment for us when we remember to remember this truth: You and I can never be closer to spirit than we are in this holy instant, we can only be more aware that we are already 100% pure spirit. When we do this consciously, we call it the practice of spirituality.

The masters have nothing on you and me except the awareness that we already have the light for which we are looking. I close with a quote from the book *Glimpse after Glimpse* written by the venerable Sogyal Rinpoche, a Buddhist monk:

> It is said that when Buddha attained enlightenment all he wanted to do was to show the rest of us the nature of mind and share completely what he had realized. But he also saw, with the great sorrow of infinite compassion, how difficult it would be for us to understand. For even though we have the same inner nature as Buddha, we have not recognized it because it is so enclosed and wrapped up in our individual ordinary minds. Imagine an empty vase. The space inside is exactly the same as the space outside. Only the fragile walls of the vase separate one from the other. Our Buddha mind is enclosed within the walls of our ordinary mind. But when we become enlightened, it is as if the vase shatters into pieces. The space "inside" merges instantly into the space "outside." They become one: There and then we realize that they were never separate or different; they were always the same.

Mindfulness Practice

↪ Practice visualizing the empty vase exercise given by Sogyal Rinpoche and notice how all sense of separation begins to dissolve.

↪ Mindfully practice presence today while you do your normal life activities, and you will witness what enlightenment is. You need go no further than the front door to be a master.

74

*A power struggle collapses when you withdraw
your energy from it. It cannot continue without
your intention to manipulate and control. When
your intention is to observe your inner process,
everything else changes. Power struggles become
uninteresting to you when you change your
intention from winning to learning about yourself.*

~Gary Zukav and Linda Francis

There can be no doubt that literally all arguments and power struggles are founded upon a need to control—it's about a need to win something. Granted, there may well be times when it seems appropriate to endure that struggle, such as when our children have a different idea of what is better for them than we do, and so on. But generally speaking, let's bottom–line it: What are all power struggles really about? They are about the fear that lies behind the feeling of powerlessness, driving it mindlessly. The fear is driven by the mistaken belief that once we are in control, we will "win" what we are all really seeking: inner peace.

The truth is that we live in a culture where power struggles are a way of life, but it doesn't have to be that way. As long as we draw our identity and sense of security and wholeness from winning our power struggles with the world, we will be placing our inner peace in the hands of others. In his book *Seat of the Soul*, Zukav points out that we are all on a quest for more power. Most of us turn outward, hoping to find it in the five-sensory world through the acquisition of things and the control of people and their opinions. Zukav refers to this as external power. He also states that more and more people are beginning to turn within, discovering their authentic power, which is where the soul self (God individuated) lives. That power can never be depleted, taken away, or lost. The obvious difference between external power and our authentic power is simple: As we learn to live from an identity of the soul self, all power struggles with the world cease. They will simply collapse because we have withdrawn our energy, which is required to sustain it.

The good news is that our authentic power has always been there. Most of us have just been looking for it in the wrong place: outside ourselves. A local bank has recently mounted a huge advertising campaign with the slogan "You Have More Power Than You Think" pasted on billboards everywhere I go. Of course, they are talking about borrowing power and my ability to put myself deeper into debt, but it has helped serve as a constant reminder that I always have a choice as to where I will turn for my power. It isn't the bank, other people, or their opinions, it is God within. Let your power struggles be done once and for all, because you really do have more power than you think. Actually, because God is all there is, you are more powerful than you think. Think about that!

Mindfulness Practice

🍂 Here is an opportunity to clarify your intentions and move from a need to win to a desire to learn more about yourself.

🍂 Have you ever found lasting inner peace through your power struggles with others? If you think you have, it is only your egoic self playing mind games with you. So, why do you continue to have power struggles? Of course, the answer is because you are afraid not to. The idea of being out of control is terrifying and so you continue the tug-of-war, hoping that inner peace will follow your victory. But even if you "win," it never does, does it?

🍂 Explore your intentions behind the next power struggle you get into (yes, unless you are a fully evolved being, it is likely you will have one or two more) and recognize the fear. Then make a conscious choice to withdraw your energy from the battle, realizing you don't have to "win" in order to have inner peace.

🍂 Would you really like to have the last word in a power struggle? Just tell the other person that they are right and then . . . smile.

75

> *We don't have to attain nirvana, because we
> ourselves are always dwelling in nirvana. The
> water does not have look for water. It already is
> water. We are one with the ground of our being.*
>
> ~Thich Nhat Hanh

The word nirvana comes from ancient Sanskrit and literally means "to blow out." My understanding of this term is that to achieve nirvana is to reach a place in our spiritual evolution where we "blow out" all sense of separation and duality where there is a total, complete, and absolute sense of unity or oneness with the all. It could be called a total merging with God.

There have been times in my life when that golden moment of nirvana seemed just one breath away. All of a sudden, I would remember an argument I recently had with a loved one, or that lower back pain would begin shooting down my leg, or the phone would ring and it would be the bank telling me my account was overdrawn, and so on. It is amazing the number of things that can pop up in any holy instant, sucking us right out of the now into duality and a sense of separation from God. What do you think it might take to "blow out" that sense of separation in any given moment, allowing us to experience our total unity with the infinite?

I suggest the next time you are near the ocean that you invite the water to be your teacher. What is required of the wave to be one with the ocean? Nothing! It already is. Likewise, what is required of you to be one with God? Nothing! You already are. God is all that is. Therefore, it is literally impossible to be separate from that which you are, even when the world tries to convince you otherwise.

Perhaps we need to make room in our "ocean" that allows arguments, back pain, and phone calls from the bank to be part of our spiritual experience. It really is all God.

Mindfulness Practice

- Take some time and dwell upon your unity with the all.

- Ask yourself, "What circumstance has created a feeling of turbulence within me?" Regardless of how choppy the water of your being may become, remember it is all God. You don't have to look for God; you are swimming in the ocean of God.

- Now, take a deep breath and let go . . . float with the waves and the circumstances of your day. Feels good, doesn't it?

76

IN SICKNESS AND
IN HEALTH

---

*Enlightenment flowers not as an ideal, but in the
miraculous reality of our human form, with its
pleasures and pains. The Buddha had illnesses and
backaches. Sages like Ramana Maharshi, Karmapa,
and Suzuki Roshi died of cancer in spite of their
holy understanding. Their example shows we must
find awakening in sickness and in health, in
pleasure and in pain, in this human body as it is.*

~Jack Kornfield

Have you ever had one (or many) of those days when your body
was not quite emanating the perfect, radiant, divine light that is
"supposed" to simply ooze out of the pores of every spiritually
enlightened being and then felt guilty for it? There was a time early in
my spiritual quest when that was exactly my experience. The truth be
known, there were a few Sundays when I would skip going to church
because I had a bad cold or an injury of some sort. Of course, my excuse
for not going was that I didn't want to inconvenience or contaminate
everyone in church, but oddly enough, it didn't keep me from going out
to a movie with about five hundred strangers on Saturday night. I was
ashamed that I wasn't living up to manifesting the perfect health I was
taught was possible for us all, and I didn't want to have that
ever-famous metaphysical guilt trip "Well, what's in your
consciousness?" hurled at me by my fellow students and teachers.
Actually, they never really said that, but I just knew they were thinking
it! Talk about projecting your own fears of inadequacy onto others—I
held a Black Belt in the art of projection.

Thank God the New Thought movement has evolved past the idea
that being enlightened means having to manifest perfection in the

physical and material world. Or is it possible that it is me who has evolved in my perspective of what spiritual perfection is and in that process has ceased to be moved by the opinions of others?

The fact is that the very body in which your soul self resides at this moment, perhaps with all of its aches and pains, is creating exactly the experience you need to be fully alive as a human being and as a spiritual being. The aliveness and real healing comes in knowing that it's through fully embracing your humanness that you find your divinity. Just about every master and mystic has had to deal with the reality and apparent limitations of the human condition. We judge far too much by appearances. To believe there is any less of God's perfect presence in a cancer ward than at a health spa is like thinking there is less of God's presence in a dandelion than a rose. The reality is that it may well be through the challenges your physical body manifests that you more fully open and awaken to the divine nature of your being. You can try and wait until everything is perfect in your life before you seek that moment of enlightenment, but you will be waiting an eternity—literally. You can chew each mouthful of brown grain rice one thousand times before you swallow it, but still one day, your body will become an unfit garment in which the soul self can reside. Take care of the temple, yes, maintain it well, but don't believe it has to be perfect in the eyes of the world before you can have the spiritual experience you came here to have.

Mindfulness Practice

✍ Take a moment right now and do a quick scan of your body. As you do, think of yourself as a soul being wearing a garment of flesh and bones.

✍ Analyze your garment and observe any areas where there may be aches and pains or simply unpleasing sensations that up until now you may have labeled as bad or as something that stood between you and your spiritual growth and wholeness.

✍ Realize that the soul being you are doesn't judge the garment as unsuitable or less than perfect in this holy instant so why should you?

✍ In sickness and in health, in pleasure and in pain, be awakened to the fact that you are 100% spirit. That's what enlightenment is. Don't wait to be the enlightened being you have come to be.

77 RELATIONSHIPS... WHO NEEDS THEM?

We are each driven by a deep urge to form an
intimate connection with the world around us and
most of us do this through relationships. If you take
a soul look at this, you will see that your need for
relationship actually stems from your basic human
need to overcome your earthly sense of separation.

~Caroline Reynolds

Play along with me in this visualization: Imagine that you are amazingly wealthy in every way. You have total freedom in your life. You live in a fifty-room mansion; drive a different luxury car of your choice each day of the week; you have the most beautiful, fit, and healthy body; you are a great athlete; and a genius to boot. In short, you have the best of everything on the planet; beyond all that, you are a truly good and wonderful human being in every way. It all sounds quite perfect, doesn't it? Now imagine that you are the only living person on the planet. This changes things a bit, doesn't it? When you stop and consider it, it's your relationships that make life truly worth living. Yes, having all of the aforementioned accoutrements may well enhance how you might function in your relationships, but it's fair to say that if you were all alone on this planet, it would get real boring real fast. We all came here hardwired to be in relationships with our partners, family, friends, and work associates as well as with the clerks in the store and strangers on the street. We need each other in order to do what we have come here to do. And what is that you might ask? We have come here to give form and expression to the life that God is. God seeks to know more of Its own divine nature, which can only happen through Its creation, as Its creation. It is in, through, and by means of our relationships that

God deepens Its own experience of Itself. There is something within each of us that knows this is true, and this is why we long for a deeper connection with other living beings. As Caroline Reynolds suggests, we are actually seeking to heal that sense of separation from our true source, God. When we awaken to this urge, remembering that God is love in its highest vibration, we can then enter into every relationship knowing that this is God, loving Itself. This awareness can transform every relationship we have into a sacred and holy one, and that is what you and I have come to do. My point is this: Every relationship you have is yet another opportunity to do God's work, to become the vessel through which love flows freely, from God . . . to God. In so doing, know that you are serving your own soul's need and desire as well—to overcome the Earth-level (egoic) thinking that finds its home stuck in a collective consciousness that breeds fear and believes in isolation, duality, and separation. Honor and cherish your relationships and don't take any of them for granted, because you would have a tough time doing what you came here to do without them.

Mindfulness Practice

- Make a commitment that for the next seven days, you will honor and somehow acknowledge every relationship you are in, from your significant other to your co-workers to the server you meet the next time you dine out.

- How will you do this? That's your choice. Be creative: Let that light shine through the loving-kindness of your words, your smiles, your hugs, your tips, and your _____ (fill in the blank).

- Remember, you have come not only to bear the light but to be the reflector as well, and that is quite impossible to do all alone. Relationships: Who needs them? We all do.

78

LAUNCHINGS AND LANDINGS: TAKE NONE OF THEM FOR GRANTED

*In all affairs it's a healthy thing now and then to
hang a question mark on the things you have long
taken for granted.*

~Bertrand Russell

On February 1, 2001, along with millions of other Americans, I sat in stunned silence as reports of the loss of the space shuttle *Columbia* began to flood in. I immediately went into prayer, knowing those incredibly brave men and women who died as their spacecraft reentered the earth's atmosphere were received peacefully into God's loving embrace. Equally so, I held their loved ones awaiting their return here on terra firma in prayer, knowing that the same God was present for them in their moments of shock and pain and the realization of their loss. Who among us ever dreamed this would happen after hundreds of launchings and landings? Truly, it was a sad day and a great tragedy for us all.

It is said that if we look deeply enough into any tragedy, we may find a shred of something redeeming, something that honors the loss and pain. This awareness came to me one morning when I kissed my wife Diane as she walked out the door, got into her car, and drove off to work. I paused for a moment and thought about the families and loved ones of those seven astronauts. In much the same way, they too had sent their loved ones "off to work," most likely taking a smooth launching and landing for granted, based on the many hundreds of successful ones they had witnessed before. While there can be no comparison between the inherent risk factors of launching our loved ones off in a space shuttle and seeing them drive a car down the street, in both cases the tendency is to take their safe return for granted. In some ways, perhaps we take far too much for granted: the homes in which we live, the country in which we live, the bodies in which we live, and the relationships in which we live. It's all a gift that can only be experienced in the moment. There is no such thing as tomorrow! When tomorrow gets here, it will be today, so we are well advised not wait till tomorrow to appreciate the gift.

I invite you to consider each moment of every day as a gift from the divine and to take none of it for granted. Take no relationship for granted, take no day for granted, take no moment for granted. This doesn't mean we should live in fear of losing any part of what is near and dear to us. It simply means we can choose to be deeply mindful of how precious the gifts are and honor the gifts with gratitude and humility. When we choose to see life this way, every day, every meal, every hug, every kiss hello as well as good-bye . . . indeed every breath we take becomes a mindfulness practice that encourages us to make our grudges and resentments short lived. Our sense of wonder and awe at the gifts make it an eternally "now" experience. Bless the launchings and the landings in your life and take none of them for granted. You'll feel more connected to life, and that's the way it's supposed to be.

Mindfulness Practice

🍂 Take time to review those areas of your life where you may tend to take things for granted. Make a list of those things and carry it with you for the next week.

🍂 Read it at least ten times a day, giving thanks for the gift.

🍂 Notice how much more alive you feel and how much more alive your relationships are.

🍂 Now, pass this message on to all of those you consider a gift in your life. That action will speak louder than the words they read.

79

Man is made or unmade by himself. By the right
choice he ascends. As a being of power, intelligence,
and love, and the lord of his own thoughts, he holds
the key to every situation.

~James Allen

Recently, I had a very stimulating conversation with a man who attends our center on Sunday mornings. He told me that I had really upset his friend when I challenged her to look at her belief system. I had suggested she might consider trying something in order to fortify her spiritual growth, and she argued that she "just couldn't" do it. I then encouraged her to begin to monitor her thinking and words, and each time she caught herself declaring "I can't," she could stop and simply change the statement to "I won't." This shift in thinking and words automatically moves us out of powerlessness and perhaps a victim mentality and into a position of authentic power and choice. Victims by definition are powerless and have no choice. And while there are certainly times when people can be true victims (e.g., child abuse, random acts of violence, etc.), we tend to use the excuse "I can't" when it really is a matter of choice. This is when we make ourselves a willing victim. There are, no doubt, many legitimate times when we may be unable to do something because we are not capable. For example, I can't fly a 747 jumbo jet, I can't have a baby, I can't lift 750 pounds over my head, and so on. However, too many of us rush to use the excuse "I can't" because it is far easier than having to deal with the possible consequences of saying "I won't." This is where we can choose to step into our true and authentic power. Consider in your own life how often you may use "I can't" as a cop-out. Have you ever been asked by another person to do something or go somewhere in which you really did not have an interest? Instead of saying, "No thanks, I choose not to," you said, "I'm sorry, but I can't" or even fabricated some excuse rather than speaking honestly. Regardless of what your motivation may be for using the "I can't" escape clause, I want you to be conscious of the power in your spoken word. The universe takes what you affirm about yourself very seriously! You may end up more powerless than you care to be. Think before you say "I can't." Why? Because every choice you make moves you closer to or further away from your true and authentic power. It is also how we evolve with conscious intention. In his great book *The Seat of the Soul*, Gary Zukav states, "Choice is the engine of our evolution . . . if you choose unconsciously, you will evolve unconsciously. If you choose consciously, you will evolve consciously." I believe now is the time we make a commitment to evolve consciously, as individuals and as a collective whole. Do you? The power of choice is the greatest gift we have been given by God, second only to the gift of life itself. Use both of these gifts consciously. In so doing, you will be stepping into your true and authentic power; you will be declaring to the universe that you are not a victim. In this day and time, that's a good place to be, isn't it?

Mindfulness Practice

➢ Place a rubber band (not too tightly) around your wrist. Listen to your words and self-talk for the next few days. When you catch yourself saying "I can't" when in actuality you know in your heart you can, snap the rubber band.

➢ Then step into your power, making a choice that reflects the awareness of a conscious evolving being.

➢ To say "I choose not to" rather than "I can't" brings an amazing amount of authentic power with it. Try it and see.

80

ARE YOUR MIND AND BODY IN THE SAME PLACE?

*Our most basic assumption is that we are the way
we see ourselves and the world is the way we see it.
We are taught to believe life should be a certain way
and we should be a certain way. When it isn't and
we aren't, we assume there's something wrong and
something should be done to fix things. Suffering
happens when we want life to be other than the way
it is.*

~Cheri Huber

It was 1:30 p.m. as I sat in my car on the freeway at a dead standstill. The traffic hadn't moved fifty feet in the previous twenty minutes. Thoughts were racing through my mind, such as "It's not supposed to be this way on the freeway at 1:30 in the afternoon. Where did all these people come from, and why aren't they at work or at home where they should be?" I was really becoming a participant in the drama when suddenly, like a Greyhound bus in the fast lane, a phrase that I read in a book by the Buddhist mystic Ram Doss came roaring through my head: "Be here now." Given the awareness that I really had no other choice, I started laughing so hard I'm sure my fellow gridlocked sojourners must have thought that I'd finally lost it. I had caught myself red-handed, failing to practice what I preach. It was a delicious moment in which I was reminded of where my inner peace and power lie, within, not on the freeway only when the conditions are just as I think they should be.

The realization I had was that my mind wanted my body to be someplace other than where it was at that instant, and I was suffering because of it. What a liberating moment that was for me. Nothing had to change but my perspective, and I was totally at peace, actually enjoying the moment, sitting in the fast lane on the freeway doing two miles per hour. Would worrying that I would be late for my appointment move traffic along any quicker? Of course not! I suspect most of us have been caught in similar conditions and have become victims of a mind–set that simply can't accept things the way they are. They're not the way they're "supposed to be," we simply didn't plan on having something happen the way it did, and so on.

In the East, there is a well-known saying that contains great wisdom: "Pain in life is a given, but suffering is a choice." Truly, suffering happens when we want life to be other than the way it is in the moment. This is not to say that there aren't times when it would be preferable to have some things different than they are. In those times, when possible, we need to be able and willing to take appropriate action or cease fretting about it. But think about it: In many circumstances, such as mine on the freeway, we make the assumption that there is something wrong. Question: Where was wrong taking place—on the freeway or in my mind? Clearly, I had no control over the tens of thousands of cars on the freeway and making it wrong for the freeway to be gridlock was a choice I made, based on my assumption that it should have been different than it was at that moment in time. The secret to inner peace is being present enough in every moment to witness how we see the world and ourselves and, accordingly, where we place our power. Think about this the next time you are on the freeway, zooming along in the fast lane at two miles per hour. Be here now!

Mindfulness Practice

- The Serenity Prayer: God grant me the serenity to accept the things I cannot change, courage to change the things I can, and wisdom to know the difference.

- Write down this amazing blessing of release and carry it with you in your wallet or purse. Tape it to the center of the steering wheel of your car and on your telephone as well.

- Be reminded that irrespective of circumstances, while you can't always change things, you can change how you choose to experience them.

- Allow these words to become your personal mantra for the next week, and notice your suffering diminishing accordingly.

81

THE "SELF" TRAVELS LIGHT-LY

The Beatles exist apart from my Self. I am not really Beatle George. Beatle George is like a suit or shirt that I once wore on occasion, and until the end of my life people may see that shirt and mistake it for me.

~George Harrison

I was working as a musician in the 1970s, and very late one night during a recording session at Capitol Records, George Harrison just sort of wandered in and sat down to listen. Since he knew the producer of the session, he decided to stay for a "few minutes." We all sat and talked, drank a few beers, and sang background harmonies together . . . for the better part of five hours. I can report to you that the above quote depicts exactly how he showed up that evening. He was not wearing his Beatles identity, he was just a guy named George, hanging out like a kid with some of his buddies in a garage band. Back then, I was just starting to get a clue about my spiritual reality, but without a doubt, George was already there. He has often been referred to as "the spiritual Beatle." Looking back at that evening, I can see why. He was totally unimpressed with his own fame. Why? Who he knew himself to be had nothing to do his name, fame, money, or for that matter, even his body. He didn't take himself too seriously because he knew who he really was . . . and who he wasn't. With that clarity, who others thought him to be didn't much matter. George Harrison had discovered the reality of the self he shared in God and thus had broken free from that which binds most people to their egoic self.

It was ironic: Here I was, a real nobody, struggling to be somebody, and there was George Harrison, a real somebody, acting like he was really nobody. I didn't get the full impact of this irony until many years later when I realized that the closer we get to identifying with our own divine nature (the self) the further we get from identifying with the trappings of the material world and the attachment to ego-based thinking.

How about you? Have you ever taken yourself a bit too seriously, thinking that who you are is actually defined by what you look like, how much talent you have (or don't have), how well known you are (or aren't), or how much money you have (or don't have)? Those are all "garments and labels" you wear during the course of your stay here on this planet, but it's not who you are. At the end of the day, when it's all said and done, you will turn all of that back in just like a car you had on lease. You aren't your name, your personality, your job, your money, your body, or even your feelings! In other words, you came in with absolutely nothing and will leave with absolutely nothing except for the karmic energy you brought along and created during your visit. The self you are is 100% God—pure light, individuated. So, you could say that the self you really are travels "light-ly." That's an amazing realization to have, isn't it? It also helps put things in perspective. So, do you see yourself as a nobody struggling to be somebody, or are you somebody (the self, individuated) who in truth knows you are nobody? I bet you'll be thinking about that one all day long.

Mindfulness Practice

Take a moment and think of all your possessions (or lack of), your assets (or lack of), your body and what it looks like, your personality, your feelings, your reputation, your talent, and your job. Do you define who you are by means of these things? In and of themselves, these things are neither good nor bad, they "just are." They serve a wonderful purpose because the self couldn't be expressed in the human condition without them. But also understand that they exist apart from the self you are.

Try now to visualize all of these things as a garment in which the true self travels through life, gaining all of the experiences you've come here to have.

Enjoy the journey, and while you may wear it well, don't get too attached to the garment—it has to be returned to the manufacturer.

82 HOW TO BE PERFECTLY IMPERFECT

Perfection is finally attained not when there is no longer anything to add but when there is no longer anything to take away, when a body has been stripped down to its nakedness.

~Antoine De Saint-Exupery

As the apprentice gazed with amazement over the shoulder of the brilliant Michelangelo working on his masterpiece, the statue of David, he asked, "How will you ever create the perfection you seek from this slab of crude marble?" The master relied, "I have to add nothing because the perfection is already there. All I must do is remove the unnecessary pieces." I don't know the source of this ancient and often told story, or even if it is true, but it certainly makes the point, doesn't it? Most of us believe there is something missing and that when we find it and add it, then we will arrive at perfection. The truth is sort of a dichotomy: When we blend our spiritual reality with our humanity, we discover that we are literally perfectly imperfect! How so? The perfection of God already lies within. We were born with it. Spiritually speaking, that makes us perfect just the way we are. Our perceived imperfections are just that: ours. Humanly speaking, we will never be perfect because we continue to judge ourselves as imperfect, flawed, and our tendency is to want to hide our perceived "flaws" from the world by covering them up with what we think the world will approve of.

When it comes to seeking perfection, I am a professional with years of training. As a matter of fact, there was a time in my life when I held a Black Belt in perfectionism! I actually consider myself among the ranks of the finest recovering perfectionists on the planet. What I

233

have learned is that perfectionism is something that consumes an incredible amount of energy. Many perfectionists are not really aware of how much this obsession runs (and perhaps ruins) their life. We are so busy trying to make everything and everyone perfect (but mostly ourselves) that we lose touch with the moment at hand. Perfectionism stems from a need to control. What do perfectionists need to control? Other people's opinions of ourselves! The mind–set is "If I can just cover up my flaws, I will be able to persuade other people that I am really all right, that I am enough. So I will put up this façade, which looks really good, to the world." So we go about, adding whatever we believe we need to the image in order to convince the world (and ourselves) that we are enough, while never reaching the conclusion that indeed we really are enough just the way we are.

There is nothing we need to add to who we are to know that we are enough, but it may be time to remove some unnecessary stuff, that is, outdated beliefs. The only flaw we may have is the mistaken idea that there is something more we must get, gain, or be in order to be okay. The truth is, you and I are enough because we are the manifestation of the divine. God is perfect, right now, just the way It is, in you and as you. So, it's not that we have something we need to cover up, but rather we have something to reveal to the world: the perfection that God is. As we embody this truth, we will see that we are perfectly imperfect—warts and all. So, if perfectionism has been an issue for you or "someone you know" (uh-huh), there is no time like the present to let go of your need to control. Release your attachment to needing the world's buy-in and approval. You will never get it anyway. Just know you are enough, even on your bad hair days!

Mindfulness Practice

Observe your actions and listen to your words today. If you catch yourself in a moment of perfectionist behavior, stop dead in your tracks, breathe deeply, and ask yourself, "Why do I need to control this _____? How will it make me feel better about myself? What inadequacy do I feel a need to cover up?"

Then, let go and let God, remembering there is nothing to conceal, only something to reveal.

83 · FINDING THE BLESSING IN BETRAYAL

Easter is not complete without loving the one who made it possible – Judas. Forgiveness becomes possible when we transcend appearances and realize that those people who represent the Judases in our lives and those qualities within ourselves that seem to have betrayed us have been the divine process growing us into Christs. It's all Love.

~Walter Starcke

There can be no doubt that Easter would be an entirely meaningless event if we didn't somehow find a way to personalize it in our lives today and every day. Perhaps the greatest lesson we can draw from the Easter story, which is often overshadowed by the principles of surrender, resurrection, and eternal life, is the fact that Judas actually played an essential role. Without the betrayal by Judas, the Easter story may have had a different ending.

While addressing the issue of forgiveness on several occasions, I recall hearing Mary Manin Morrissey say, "Before there could be a resurrection, there had to be a betrayal." What a powerful realization to have when it comes to forgiveness! There are very few among us who have fully mastered the issue of forgiveness. Perhaps our personal resurrection, that is to say, our ability to be born anew to this day, free and clear of an unhealthy past, has been retarded by our attachment to resentment and nonforgiveness. Is it really possible to see that those who have betrayed us were actually playing a necessary role in our spiritual growth and evolution? That's exactly what Jesus did with Judas. Jesus knew that betrayal by Judas was essential for his full ascension to Christhood. Can you imagine Jesus, during his trial before Pilate, saying "I just can't believe Judas did

236

that to me . . . after all I did for him . . . .How could he betray me . . . that dirty rotten rat, he has hurt me deeply . . . I am really mad now, and I will never ever forgive him for what he has done to me"? Of course, we can't imagine that kind of a scene because Jesus knew only good could come from that betrayal; it opened the door to his own personal resurrection and the final healing of any sense of separation from God. Forgiveness does that.

How about you? Is there any need for forgiveness in your life today? First, have you ever betrayed yourself? Most of us have at some time or another. Perhaps that's where forgiveness needs to start—with yourself. Second, are you ready to rise above and transcend any attachment you have to what someone else may have done that they "shouldn't have" and accept the idea that somehow they were playing an essential role in your own spiritual evolution? This can be a tough one, and it will be impossible to accomplish if you insist on maintaining a victim consciousness. Jesus never saw himself as a victim because he chose to see the blessing in the betrayal, and he knew that forgiveness was as necessary as the betrayal itself. When you and I can have that same Christ perspective, we will discover that the one we haven't forgiven in our heart is the one who will actually assist us the most in moving forward on our journey toward living fully in the light of God. Walter Starcke is right: Bless the Judases in your life—it's all love.

Mindfulness Practice

➤ Search your heart today and see if you discover any resentment, either toward yourself or others, that is attached to a sense of betrayal.

➤ Knowing that betrayal represents a violation of trust, dig deeply enough within to realize that through this violation, you are being given the opportunity to heal a false belief of separation between you and God.

➤ Forgiveness is how you do it. Release your betrayer unto the law of their own being.

➤ Trust that life will support you in transcending the past, irrespective of how hurtful it has been. Now, take a deep breath, let go, and let God.

84

BECOME THE DE-TERMINATOR

The longer I live, the more I am certain that the difference between the great and the insignificant is energy – invincible determination – a purpose once fixed, and then death or victory.

~Sir Thomas Fowell Buxton

I'm always on the lookout for real-life examples of people who demonstrate exemplary character from which we can learn and grow. One such story unfolded when a young mountaineer named Aron Ralston became pinned by the arm underneath an eight-hundred-pound boulder in a remote Utah canyon. After five days with no sign of help, this man did the unthinkable, amputating his own arm below the elbow . . . with a dull pocketknife! Then, after the "surgery," he had the clarity of mind and the strength of body to rig a harness, rappel down a sixty-foot cliff, and hike out to safety. Can you imagine the focus and determination this amazing man must have had to pull this off? When asked how he did it, his reply was, "I felt pain and I coped with it." I don't know about you, but this really makes me reevaluate my resistance to going to the dentist! Aron's story is living proof that when the chips are down, a human being can do just about anything with determination and a clear sense of focus on the end result, which in his case, was simply staying alive. When he determined that dying was not an option, something indestructible emerged from within him. You could say he became "The De-Terminator" like Arnold Schwarzenegger in the movie. Something non-human kicked in and lifted Aron above his fear and pain, giving him the clarity, power, and courage to do what he had to do. Of course, we know that something non-human is pure essence, God, the unlimited power of spirit and mind. Irrespective of whether Aron knew it or not, he had summoned the greatest power in the universe, accessing two inherent qualities that determine our life experience: intention (born in the intellect) backed by desire (born in the heart). He intended to live to a long life, and his desire to do so made it a reality, guiding and empowering him to take the appropriate action in the moment to ensure that his intention would happen. To draw value from this lesson, it's vital to understand that the intention and desire came from within him not outside him, and his determination tied the two together. Thankfully, most of us have never been rendered helpless by an eight-hundred-pound boulder, but at one time or another, nearly all of us have felt emotionally pinned down or encumbered by some situation, condition, or event. The point is that the same power that got Aron Ralston through his ordeal also resides within each of us, waiting to be summoned. We don't have to wait for help to arrive—it's already there, at the core of who we are. It's our divine potential. It is the intelligence, strength, wisdom, creativity, genius, unlimited power, and unformed essence of God, and there is no limit to what It can do. However, God can only do for us that which God can do through us. We have to be the conduit through which It reveals Itself. In Aron's case, it was his own invincible determination and strong sense of purpose in that moment that brought that potential forward. So, if there are any "boulders of burden" holding you down today, consider becoming "The De-Terminator": Choose to determine your own future rather than be a victim of circumstances. How? Develop the determination to fix your attention on the power that is greater than the egoic you, which dwells at the very core of your being. Then realize that your soul purpose in every moment is to seek a fuller expression of the life that God gave you, knowing that nothing can impede that power—nothing! It just needs to be called upon, and it is your determination that places the call. Aron Ralston made the call and so can you and I.

Mindfulness Practice

- Do you feel trapped by any boulders of burden in your life today? What is holding you down that you need to be free of in order to honor the life you have come to live?

- With great determination, align yourself with "whatever is" in this moment and consciously experience the presence of God moving through you as spirit. It knows how to sustain you as mind, thinking clearly, revealing exactly what you need to do, and as body, responding with calm certainty, taking action, doing what needs to be done.

- Trust that the divine intelligence that goes with you into the canyons of life knows how to get you out of them too.

85

YOU ARE ONE OF
A KIND, LIKE IT
OR NOT!

Originality consists in trying to be like everybody
else – and failing.

~Raymond Radiguet

Recently, I read about an experiment involving the first attempt to clone a cat. The researchers were somewhat baffled by the fact that the original cat, Rainbow, is a typical calico with very distinct markings, and the clone, Cc, looks totally different in color and patterns. Further, Rainbow has a large chunky body, whereas Cc is thin and sleek. But most interesting of all, is that Rainbow's personality is very reserved and introverted, while Cc is overtly curious and playful. By the way, these comparisons were made after Cc was fully grown. The point of all this is that regardless of how hard the scientists tried, they failed miserably at re–creating the exact same cat.

Scientists may be able to extract DNA from anything that has a material density or body, and while they may be able to manipulate it in a manner that serves the needs of the world in many wonderful ways, they will never be able to re-create the essence, character, and life force that dwells at the center of and animates all living things. While this may be disappointing news for pet owners who understandably want to re-create their favorite pet, it confirms the fact that God, in Its infinite wisdom and creative nature, is incapable of being redundant. The fact is that even if they could clone a physical human body that would be identical to the original, the soul self that indwells the body would have to be unique and different, and the personality and character tendencies would have to reflect those differences. As I understand the divine intent of God, Its desire is to express and experience Itself through and as Its creation. To create any two forms of expression that are exactly the same would be redundant and counterproductive to the evolutionary, upward spiraling motion that propels all life. This is good information to keep in mind the next time we catch ourselves trying to emulate, impersonate, or re-create ourselves in someone else's image, isn't it?

The point of my message this: Be yourself. Be who you have come to be and let go of the idea that any other person is better equipped than you to give form and expression to God's life. You have been chosen by the infinite to be you! You are unique and one of a kind whether you like it or not, and it is actually dishonoring the gift of life to try and clone yourself after another. Do you know what the primary difference is between you and me and between Rainbow and Cc? I doubt that they look at each other and then judge themselves as being less than purrrrrfect just the way they are. However, we tend to do that, don't we? Today, give some thought to what an amazing thing it is to have been given the gift of life with which to be a unique and beautiful expression of the divine. Don't dishonor the gift by trying to be like anyone else. You aren't and never can be. That's the real beauty of it . . . and the real gift!

Mindfulness
Practice

🍂 Find a mirror into which you can look for a good length of time and simply begin to gaze into your own eyes. As you look into your eyes, ask yourself, "Who is in there?" Ponder this question as you go deeper.

🍂 Keep looking until you get past all the layers of judgment based on appearance . . . the color and condition of the skin and eyes . . . the hair that's growing where you don't want it to and not growing where you think it should . . . .Peel off the layers as if you were an onion.

🍂 As you go deeper into this exercise, you will discover that the unique being gazing back at you is nothing less than God. This is God, looking at Itself, loving Itself, intentionally expressing Itself in you, through you, and as you just the way you are. Marvel in how perfectly unique you really are and give thanks it was meant to be so. Then, smile at that being and say "Namaste!"

APPRECIATE THE GIFT

Appreciation of life itself, becoming suddenly aware
of the miracle of being alive, on this planet, can
turn what we call ordinary life into a miracle. We
come awake to such a realization when we recognize
our connection to a spiritual dimension.

~Dan Wakefield

I am just now coming out of a weeklong physical challenge, having dealt with a nasty little virus that snuck up on me and really whacked me upside the head. The most startling part about this for me was that I never get sick. So, for the better part of five days, I was doing that metaphysical self-analysis thing. You know, the guilt trip, seeking the cryptic cause of the negative experience, blah, blah, blah. It's a pointless exercise in feeling rotten about feeling rotten, but it seems that on special occasions, we all have the tendency to get out the hammer and start pounding. Fortunately, my prayer partner called me and pulled me out of that nosedive. As I regained my sense of God's ever presence, my mind began to focus on something a bit more productive, and in the process of evicting this visiting virus, I consciously invited it to be my master teacher of the moment. However, the lesson I sought was not about what was in my consciousness to create such an experience but rather what I missed out on in my life while I was busy feeling rotten about feeling rotten.

Here was my awareness: As I sat down this morning to write about these thoughts, I noticed a large vase full of beautiful roses sitting right there next to my computer monitor. My wife Diane has a talent for growing flowers, and I thought this was a lovely gift, her way of beautifying my office after a week of me hacking, drooling, spitting, and coughing all over the place. (I know, that's gross, huh? That's what she said too.) Well, I went to thank her for her thoughtfulness and told her that they would really brighten up my day! She looked at me, paused, and smiled curiously, saying "I put those roses there four days ago, honey." Four days ago! Now, that would not be such a bad thing had I not been sitting at my computer off and on for all those days, doing much of my usual business. Granted, I was a little less focused than normal, but nonetheless, there they were, glorious roses, in full bloom right in front of my nose. Had I not been so busy feeling rotten about feeling rotten, perhaps I might have seen the roses earlier and enjoyed them even more.

Life is like that, isn't it? We can have the most glorious and beautiful gifts stuck right under our noses every day, but if we become overly preoccupied with the challenges that life is guaranteed to present, we never see the gift that lies in the moment at hand. In truth, we don't need to be stricken with the inconvenience of a virus or other more serious maladies to be oblivious to the gifts of the moment, do we? Do you ever get to feeling badly that things seem to be going poorly in some area of your life? Do you ever get so caught up in the drama of what's unfolding that you lose sight of the gifts that life is laying at your feet in every holy instant? If you do, stop and think about my roses. The gift was made long before I was ready to enjoy it; what a waste of that beauty! The beautiful gifts that life brings us every day are beyond measure, but we have to be willing to be present enough in the moment to see them. What gift has been laid at your feet today? Perhaps now would be a great time to stop, look down, and appreciate it, because as with my roses, it may not be there forever. Appreciate the gifts that life brings you in every moment. You deserve them.

Mindfulness Practice

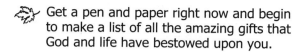 Get a pen and paper right now and begin to make a list of all the amazing gifts that God and life have bestowed upon you.

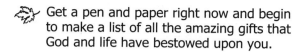 Start with the gifts you have become so used to that you tend to take them for granted (e.g., a bed on which to sleep, food to eat, electricity to light up your home).

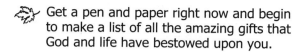 Continue to develop this list over the next few days and notice how much more present you are in every moment, even when the inconveniences of the moment beckon your attention.

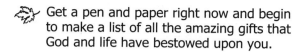 Begin to be aware—the greatest gift of all is the gift of life itself. Appreciate every holy instant of it!

87   HOW WILL YOU LIVE?

We are getting closer to death with every breath,
and no strategy will exempt us from a sure and
certain end to our life as we know it. Does this make
us depressed? On the contrary, it can set us
free — free from the illusion that one more phone
call, one more meeting, another hundred dollars
will buy us safety, happiness, immortality. It is all
chasing after the wind. When we stop chasing the
wind, we can begin to live in peace.

~Wayne Muller

In his wonderful book *How Then, Shall We Live?*, one of the profound questions Wayne Muller challenges his readers to ask themselves is "How shall I live, knowing I will die?" This is one of the most powerful exercises we can ever do for ourselves—to actually take time to pause and consider the reality that we will indeed one day die. It could be in seventy years, seven years, seven days, or seven minutes. This is a rich question to entertain because it could well alter the way we live the rest of our lives.

I believe that most of us avoid asking ourselves this question because we don't like the idea that it will all one day come to an end. The result of this mind–set often leads us to live shallow lives, where the roots of our being are never allowed to sink deeply into the rich sacredness of the moment and the deeper meaning of our existence here. All because we are living (perhaps unconsciously) in fear of our pending death rather than in spite of it. The result is that we hold back from living life fully in the moment. All because we have not made peace with the inevitable: That which has a beginning must have an end. There are two realities here. We know our spiritual being is eternal. Its essence is rooted in the Allness of God. It always has been and always shall be. And, conversely, we know our physical being, which had an obvious beginning, will one day cease to be. The question we have to ask ourselves is, From which reality do we draw our identity and live our lives?

Too often, we put off living fully today because we are living "fear-fully" for tomorrow. Until we are free of our fear of the unknown and the fear of this illusion called death, we shall never be free to fully live in the present, which is really all we have. We will continue to hold the best of who we are back from life and from those we love. This fear will keep us from doing and being what we have come here to do and be. It will deprive us of what we are all seeking the most: full expression and inner peace, a peace that can only be found in each holy instant. No matter how much we do to avoid this reality, it is the truth. As Wayne Muller infers, our efforts to avoid the inevitable by staying busy with the minutiae of life is like chasing the wind. Stop chasing the wind and ask yourself how you shall live from this day forward. Then get busy doing it. I invite you to take the mindfulness practice to heart. It could change the meaning and purpose of the rest your life, irrespective of how short or long it may be.

Mindfulness Practice

- Think on this question today: If you knew your physical life was going to end in seven days, how would you live those seven days?

- Where would your priorities be?

- Would you rush off to the office and make sure that your desk is neat and clean and that the in-basket is empty?

- Or, would you make more time to share the sacred space of your life with God and your most cherished loved ones?

- Would you get out into the community and finally find a place to make a difference?

- Would you be more aware of how you speak to strangers as well as loved ones?

- Would you be more mindful of how you treat those whom you may have taken for granted in the past?

- The fact is you might only have seven days to live, or for that matter seven hours. So, the question really is, How then shall you live today, knowing you will die?

88

SPIRITUAL FITNESS: JOURNEY OR DESTINATION?

Spirituality is not about being perfect but about aspiring to a life of heart-filled integrity. It is a journey and not a destination. When we are spiritually fit and balanced we are a powerfully exquisite blend of human fallibility and divine perfection. It is this dynamic tension that gives us our uniqueness, our power to create and our compassion.

~Caroline Reynolds

When I first picked up Caroline Reynolds book and saw the title, *Spiritual Fitness*, I instantly visualized a very sacred spiritual master, advanced in years but built like Arnold Schwarzenegger doing curls with a 450-pound dumbbell with one hand while meditating at the same time. When you think of being spiritually fit, what images come to your mind? I know my example is silly, but let's face it: Taking charge of our spiritual fitness is probably as challenging for most of us as maintaining optimum physical fitness is. I don't know about you, but there are days when I simply don't feel motivated to get out there and jump on the ol' treadmill or do the stretching I know is so vital to my physical well-being. Likewise, there are days when I look for any excuse I can find to avoid sitting down and doing my spiritual discipline. I wonder if sometimes we have such high ideals set in our minds as to what spiritual fitness is "supposed" to look like that we feel defeated before we even begin, so we find ways to put off ever beginning. In the process, we end up living an out-of-balance life because of some mistaken belief we have been told along the way that spirituality is about always being perfect. While the spirit that we are is indeed perfect, practicing our awareness of its presence is never quite so.

As Caroline Reynolds suggests, it's not about finding the unobtainable perfection in the human experience but rather seeking the perfect blend between the human and the divine. It's not about what you do so much as it is who you are in your day-to-day dealings. Spiritual fitness helps get us there! She offers six questions we can ask ourselves to see how spiritually fit we are: (1) How loving and kind am I? (2) How free am I? (3) How honest am I? (4) How wise am I? (5) How at peace am I? (6) How joyful am I?

Notice that not even one of the questions refers directly to practicing spirituality, but in truth, they all reflect the actions of someone who is deeply connected to life—someone who is spiritually fit. Think about it: You know that when you are anchored in your spiritual truth, loving-kindness is a way of life because you have developed reverence for all life. When you live mindfully, remembering that God is your source, you are truly free because you are not dependent on others for your good or for their approval. When you integrate a conscious awareness of spirit's presence in every area of your life, you begin to live authentically with spiritual integrity. Honesty is simply the action of living with integrity. And, when you listen to the divine knower within, that natural inherent wisdom guides you with grace and ease through your life 24/7, which has to manifest as inner peace. Finally, when you live in an awareness of God's presence, the spirit within lifts you in authentic joy, which is infectious because you have risen above the belief in duality and fear. That's also when you live life more boldly.

This is what spiritual fitness looks like in action, and the key to remember is that while you don't have to be perfect or an ascended master to practice spiritual fitness, there are two things you absolutely do have to be: awake and willing. Being spiritually fit is not a place of destination at which we one day arrive; it is a journey of a lifetime for the awake and willing, and it begins with your first step, even if it isn't perfect.

Mindfulness Practice

- Take time right now to reread the six questions that serve as the cornerstones for living a life that is based in spiritual fitness. Be as real with your answers as possible.

- As you ask yourself the questions and be aware of what your body is reporting to you. If you get a "click" within that says there is room to grow in a certain area, you will know where to start your fitness program.

- See how you can incorporate a greater awareness of God's presence in that area of your life, and then move on to the next, and then the next.

- Don't look for perfection, look for that exquisite blend of the human and the divine. Enjoy the journey!

89

MAKE THE WORLD A BETTER PLACE— CHOOSE TO BE HAPPY!

The purpose of life is the expansion of happiness.

~Maharishi Mahesh Yogi

Several years ago, we were blessed to have Don Miguel Ruiz, the author of *The Four Agreements*, come to our center and present a seminar. While dining with him prior to his presentation, I asked what I thought was a profound question, "What is our purpose in life?" As he took a slow and deliberate drink of water, I prepared myself for a long and intense, deeply profound answer. His three-word response sort of took my breath away. "To be happy," was all he said. My first thought (which I wisely kept to myself) was "Golly, Don Miguel, that sounds awfully self-serving . . . with the world being in the condition it is today and all . . . that's it? Our purpose in life is to . . . just 'be happy'"? Well, knowing that I was in the presence of a master, I just nodded, smiled, and decided to wait and see what would be revealed in my awareness as I let this idea percolate for a while. I observed him throughout the evening, and indeed, I saw a man who seemed to be very happy in a quiet sort of way, regardless of whether he was sitting alone by himself, with one person, or with several hundred people. The one thing that was overwhelmingly obvious was the genuine love that flowed through him at all times—it was palpable. I have seen him several times since then, and he has always been consistently happy and loving.

Being happy and loving seem to go together quite well, don't they? That night with Don Miguel caused me to simplify my spiritual practices greatly. Have you ever thought of happiness as a spiritual practice that honors your purpose here? Just about every picture I have ever seen of his holiness the Dalai Lama shows him laughing or with a big smile on his face. Think about it. When you are busy being genuinely happy, it's pretty hard to be mean spirited, cruel, judgmental, violent, hateful, resentful, petty, or selfish. That's because in that moment of happiness, a great generosity of spirit (love) surges and expands upon itself through us, lifting us above the energy of fear, which is a lower vibration. Even if we don't recognize that moment as a spiritual experience, it is. And the best part of it is that it affects others in the most positive ways too. Truly, the purpose of life really is the expansion of happiness, and you and I are the vessels through which it can happen.

So, the larger question is, Where do we find happiness? Unfortunately, the common belief with most people is that happiness is something that happens to them when conditions are just right rather than something that happens through them when they choose to make space for it. While outer conditions may stimulate the feeling of happiness, it can never come from anywhere other than within us. Authentic happiness isn't something we can go out and get, buy, borrow, or steal. Nor can any form of artificial sensory stimulus generate true happiness; it's only something we can be, and it's a choice we make with every breath we take. We just need to make space in our minds and heart for happiness to be revealed. So, breathe into this moment and choose to be happy. Given the alternative, it's a wise thing to do. A wise man, this Don Miguel Ruiz.

Mindfulness Practice

- Generally, when you are unhappy, you will discover it's because you either want something you don't have, have something you don't want, or are simply too attached to something you do have. Choose a different perspective today— choose to be happy with what is and stop putting off being happy until things change.

- Start by focusing on what is right and good about your life in this holy instant and breathe into it.

- Choose to be happy . . . the world will be a better place because of it!

90

STEPPING INTO THE MYSTERY OF "I DON'T KNOW"

Part of a commitment to living in the mystery more of the time means learning to become more comfortable swimming in a sea of questions rather than standing rigidly on islands of concrete beliefs, especially about things that are beyond our capacity to know without absolute certainty.

~Dr. Jordan Paul

Have you ever read a good mystery novel that really had you wondering "who done it" until the very end of the book? Somehow, the author kept you involved throughout the entire story by not giving you the answer you were seeking. In much the same way, life is a mystery too. The only difference is that when it comes to life, we often have a far greater attachment to knowing how the story is going to end long before it does, and we suffer greatly because of it. Whether we are talking about our lives, our relationships, our careers, or any other aspect of our daily existence, most of us are greatly attached to knowing (controlling) in advance exactly how everything is going to turn out. And, because of this, we live smaller, condensed, fearful little lives. If you stop and consider this, it's really quite something. Life truly is the ultimate mystery: We are born from the pure essence of divine creation, given a body in which we rattle around for a given period of time, and then we leave again, going back into the divine essence from which we came. That, in and of itself, is AMAZING! What a miracle . . . what a mystery! The space between those two points is what we refer to as "life," and we spend most of it trying to figure out why things are the way they are and how we can manipulate, control, and squeeze more out of it rather than living in awe of the sweetness of the mystery itself.

Life is a mystery, and those who insist on knowing the whys and hows of everything are not generally happy and peaceful individuals. That's because their need to know is driven by fear and insecurity not inspiration. The bottom line is that some things are simply beyond our capacity to know with absolute certainty; to try and do so will make our experience here very unsettling. We are here to evolve, giving a deeper and fuller expression to the life that God is. That requires us to continually push out further into the mystery of the unknown, stepping out of "I have to know" and into "I don't know." Believe it or not, that's also where we connect with authentic inner peace. There is an amazing release that happens when we let go of the need to know it all. When we can live in wonderment, not just by accepting what is but by being willing to see infinite intelligence at work, a deep and profound peace accompanies it.

Of course, the pathway on which we walk that enables us to step into the mystery of "I don't know" is faith. What does it really mean to have faith? In Hebrews 11:1, it is stated with such simple elegance that it cannot easily be misunderstood: "Faith is the substance of things hoped for, the evidence of things not seen." In other words, it's possible to hold space in your heart that includes a willingness to allow life to support you in your forward movement without being attached to how it will do so. That's a profound thought, isn't it? So, hold a vision for yourself and what your life can be but be willing to take the action of faith, because faith without works really is dead. Ultimately, this requires you to step into "I don't know" without an agenda other than to be in awe of the mystery itself, understanding that contained within the mystery is what you need to truly be the evolving being you've come to be. Ah, sweet mystery of life . . .

Mindfulness Practice

Take some time to explore the mystery of life. Look into another person's eyes until you see only God gazing back.

Look into the blossom of a flower until you see the perfection of the design and realize who created it.

Think about the meal you last had and be in absolute wonder of how that food is now being turned into fingernails, skin, organs, and hair.

After you have done all these things, ask yourself, "How did God do all that?" Of course, the answer will be "I don't know." Feel the peace that comes with that awareness.

Finally, contemplate something that you have recently been seeking to know or understand that has caused you to feel unsettled. Remembering the awe and peace you felt just by contemplating the mystery of life, step into "I don't know" again and trust that God does know. Have faith that, at this moment, that's all you need to know.

91

*The first agreement: Be impeccable with your word.
Speak with integrity and say only what you mean.
Through the word you express your creative power.
Regardless of what language you speak, your intent
manifests through your word.*

~Don Miguel Ruiz

Don Miguel Ruiz's suggestion that we "be impeccable with our word" is by far one of the most powerful ways to ensure that our lives remain in spiritual integrity. In truth, our word is far more than what comes out of our mouths, it represents what we stand for. In and of themselves, our words are but symbols that represent our intentions. Sometimes, we have a tendency to say things we don't really mean. That holds true both for some of the less than loving things we might say to others in a heated moment of thoughtlessness as well as those people-pleasing moments when we give compliments that are not really sincere. In addition, sometimes people make commitments and promises to others never intending to keep them.

My point is this: Irrespective of what we are saying and to whom we are saying it, quite often the words don't really symbolize what the underlying intent is. However, the reality is that in either case, we are still using the power of our word (backed by intention) to declare to the universe what we stand for. The universe doesn't hear words, it senses our feelings and the intention behind the words . . . and says yes to our intentions. Therefore, if our intentions are dishonorable or simply cloudy and confused, it has to show up in the body of our relationships. To be impeccable in our word is to bring our spoken word and our unspoken intention into alignment so that the inner thought and the outer action are the same. When this happens, we find ourselves living in true spiritual integrity, actually integrating the awareness of God's presence into not just our words but our intentions and actions as well.

With your intentions and words, what will you declare to the universe you stand for today? See the next section for the second agreement.

Mindfulness Practice	➤ Become an impartial observer of your own thoughts and words and be keenly aware of what the intention is behind the words you say.
	➤ If you find yourself saying one thing while thinking or feeling another, stop and realign with God in that holy instant.
	➤ Don't compromise your integrity by being less than impeccable with your word. You will discover you like the person gazing back at you in the mirror even more.

92

WHAT YOU THINK OF ME

The second agreement: Don't take anything
personally. When you are immune to the opinions
and actions of others, you won't be the victim of
needless suffering.

~Don Miguel Ruiz

A student went to his master teacher and asked to know the key to true inner peace and freedom from emotional suffering. The master said to him, "Go to the cemetery and curse the person that lay in each grave. Tell them that they are stupid and their mother is ugly too. After you have done that then go back again the next day and bless and praise each person in every grave, telling them how wonderful they are . . . .Tell them that the world worships them to this day . . . even go so far as to light incense and candles for each one, calling them saints. When you have done this, come back to me." The student dutifully did as instructed. Upon returning, the master asked the student, "Well, what did they have to say about your opinions?" Astounded, the student replied, "How could they respond to me at all? They were all dead and could not hear a word I said, negative or positive." The master said, "When you, too, do not hear what others have to say about you, negative or positive, you will know true inner peace and freedom from suffering."

Isn't it interesting to watch our ego get in the way when we buy in and attach to what other people think and say about us? Why do you suppose that is? At some level, we still have not accepted the fact that we really are okay just the way we are, so we develop a need (addiction) for other people's criticism or praise to prove to ourselves that how we feel about ourselves is correct. The law of attraction will always guarantee an ample supply of these individuals to assist us in demonstrating how we feel about ourselves. We find symbiotic relationships and encounters that help our ego feed on the worthlessness we feel.

The fact is that other people's opinions are never really about you, they are about themselves. We always serve as divine mirrors for one another. Dr. Terri Cole Whitaker summarized it all beautifully in the title of her book *What You Think of Me Is None of My Business*. When you are mindful of your true divine nature, other people's opinions (nice or nasty) are meaningless, because you know who you really are and have no need to be defined by people who are constantly seeking targets to project their own sense of pain and lack on. This doesn't mean that you have to ignore compliments and constructive input from others, just be sure it does not become food for the ego. By living in full awareness of God's presence, it will automatically make you immune to opinions targeted at the ego self. Make a decision not to take anything personally . . . and then notice the inner peace that comes with that release.

Mindfulness Practice	If you find that others want to offer their opinion of you today, positive or negative, smile and say, "Thanks for sharing."
	If it is negative, let it become as water off a duck's back.
	If it is positive, silently give credit where credit is due by saying to yourself, "It is not me, but God within that does the work."

93   TO ASSUME...

The third agreement: Don't make assumptions.
Find the courage to ask questions and to express
what you really want. Communicate with others as
clearly as you can to avoid misunderstandings,
sadness and drama.

~Don Miguel Ruiz

Once while hiking in the mountains, a man observed two other men across the valley also walking along a narrow pathway. They were just far enough away that he could hear them talking but could only make out the muffled sound of their voices. All of a sudden, one of the men turned to the other, shouted angrily at the top of his voice, and then violently shoved his companion off the pathway. The man rolled down the steep embankment to the bottom of the ravine unharmed. Because of his perspective and his rush to a conclusion, the observer assumed that he had just witnessed a violent act, but what he didn't see was the huge rattlesnake the man was about to step on before his friend bravely pushed him out of harm's way. What he didn't hear were the words of an impassioned warning. He assumed that they were words of anger.

Isn't it interesting how most of us tend to make assumptions about other people and situations before we have actually gathered all of the needed information? In fact, when we make an assumption we are really passing judgment without knowing all the details. This is why communication plays such a vital role in all healthy relationships. How often do we assume that the other person knows what we know or knows what we need or desire to have happen when in fact we are not all psychic? The result of this is often misplaced anger or resentment. How often have we assumed (judged) another person's behavior as unacceptable only to later learn that they were in great pain of some sort? Let's make a sincere effort to garner all the details before we reach a conclusion.

Mindfulness Practice

- Step into that place of conscious awareness where you become the impartial observer.

- If you catch yourself making assumptions throughout the day, ask yourself, what information do I need before I form an opinion regarding this issue? Then act accordingly rather than reacting based on what appears to be.

- Watch and see how the trauma **drama** becomes authentically mellow.

94

GIVE IT YOUR
PERSONAL BEST

---

*The fourth agreement: Always do your best. Your
best is going to change from moment to moment.
Under any circumstance, always do your best, and
you will avoid self-judgment, self-abuse and regret.*

~Don Miguel Ruiz

As I picked up my daughter from high school, it was obvious to me
that she was very stressed out. It seemed that she was
encountering some challenges in not one but several of the classes in
which she had previously been getting stellar grades. It appeared that
her GPA might even dip a little. She was not a happy camper about
this. It was then that I reminded her of a conversation we have had on
many occasions over the years. Since she was born, I have always told
her, "I don't care what you accomplish in school, sports, or any other
area of your life as long as you can always look into the mirror and
honestly say you've done the best you knew how to do at that time."
With that reminder, she drew a deep breath, sighed, and smiled. She
just needed a reminder of what she already knew.

Now, I invite you to also take a deep breath and sigh a little. Each
day of your life is different from the day before, so it's unrealistic to
think that your performance will be (or should be) exactly the same
every day. For some people, just making it out of bed on certain days
may be the best they can do, and that's okay. Your best may change
from day to day, moment to moment. If you are addicted to excelling
every day, you will indeed suffer greatly with self-judgment, abuse,
and regret. (As a recovering perfectionist, I am qualified to say this!)
Even God took a day off!

Likewise, if you are addicted to loafing, this may be a call for you to live up to your potential as well. In either case, there is an observer within you that knows when you are giving the best you've got in every holy instant and when you are not. Just go look in the mirror, you will see it staring back at you. Do your best each day, and you will like who you see.

Mindfulness Practice	
	Begin by looking into the mirror right now. What does that being staring back at you report? Are you giving your best effort to life today?
	Forget about the past, it is done and over. How about right now . . . are you doing the best you can in this holy instant?
	Regardless of how it may look to others, if the answer is "yes," then take a deep breath, sigh, and smile.
	If the answer is "no," the good news is your next task is just a heartbeat away.

CREATING THE CRACKS

_Am I willing to give up what I have in order to be
what I am not yet? Am I able to follow the spirit of
love into the desert? It is a frightening and sacred
moment. There is no return. One's life is changed
forever. It is the fire that gives us our shape._

~Mary Caroline Richards

As you mature spiritually, gaining new insights in life is sort of like spotting a crack in the wall of the room in which you are living. You may not be certain what it is, but something about that crack in the wall compels you to come closer. As you move closer to the crack and gaze through it, you catch just a hint of a bright light shining from an adjacent room in which you have never before set foot. It is not known what you shall find there until you actually step into the room and look; that trickle of light only makes it more intriguing. The question is, Will you explore that room or not? So it is with our spiritual growth. The light of God's presence within seeks cracks in our everyday lives through which It may shine. It is always beckoning us to be more intimate with It. It does, however, require that we leave the comfort of the room we find so familiar.

What I have discovered is that for any one of us to have an authentic deepening of our sense of the sacred, we must be willing to step into the unknown. We must let go of truths that we currently hold on to (cling to), make space in consciousness for the revelation of something more, something deeper, wider, higher, and perhaps even less tangible. This requires great faith. Indeed, to be asked to give up that which we have securely sequestered away in our mind as the only truth, as the only way it can be, is scary. Welcome to the spiritual path. Why is it so scary? Because once we have tasted the sweet nectar of a deeper truth, we can never turn back and settle for the way it used to be. And it never ends because there will always be a deeper truth to discover—more rooms to explore!

This is why some people who cling tightly to their religious beliefs argue so desperately to convince others that theirs is the right religion; it is safer for them! To even entertain the possibility that there might be another way, a deeper way, to relate with the infinite would devastate them. Perhaps it's time to reconsider the amazing wisdom of the great teacher when he said, "In my Father's house there are many rooms" (John 14:2). The truth is that every day offers opportunities to allow some light to shine through the cracks of the wall called our belief system into the unexplored rooms where our spiritual nature dwells, waiting patiently for us to enter and be more of who we have come here to be. So, be excited and look for the cracks!

Mindfulness Practice

⟫ Are you willing to give up what you have (or are holding on to) in order to be what you are not yet being?

⟫ What you have, of course, are certain beliefs that shape you and the life you see in front of you. Take time to explore what this means to you personally.

⟫ Where are you stuck? Just by looking at this, you will begin to create the cracks through which new light may begin to radiate throughout your entire being.

I hate quotations.

~Ralph Waldo Emerson

I really had a good chuckle when I was reminded of Emerson's quote above. I mean, here I am, writing inspirational messages using a different quote to begin each of my writings! So, with good intention, I quote Emerson who states that he hates quotations. While I find this both extremely humorous and ironic, it does make me wonder what would cause him to make such a statement. There can be no doubt that he was a real individualist. To make my point, I quote Emerson one more time (sorry Ralph). He said, "Imitation is suicide." Now that makes it pretty clear, doesn't it? The message he was asking us to embrace is, Be your own person, think for yourself, be an original, an authentic thinker not a duplicate. While I have always looked at quoting others not only as a compliment but also as a way to draw on their wisdom, I never considered it metaphoric suicide. Perhaps Emerson felt that by using the words (and ideas) of others too readily, we are shortchanging our own creative expression and unique inner wisdom. I would like to offer an alternative perspective: Is it possible that we are simply relating to what others say because those same ideas already lie inherent within us but have not yet found the proper avenue of expression? I believe the latter is true. If the idea didn't live within us already, there would be no essence with which to resonate in the words of another person. At some level, there must be a common knowing. The mere fact that one person's words can excite that place in another where the "yes, I agree" lives is amazing!

I recall a conversation about this I had with Gary Zukav many years ago. When I asked him how he liked being quoted so often, he said, "Don't bother quoting me, because if my words resonate with your heart, simply embrace them as your own and use them as your own, because at that point they are." My understanding of what he was saying was that words are only symbols; they are not all that important. It's the feeling, meaning, intention, and essence behind the words that matter. These are the intangible qualities that live as seeds of potential within all of us. When we hear another person's words that resonate with us, it is the divine intelligence of infinite wisdom within us saying, "Yes, while there may be two (or two thousand) of us here, we are all one in mind, and we share the same information."

I know from conversations I have had with many of my peers over the past year that a number of them use my writings in their sermons and classes. A greater compliment I could never receive, and yet if I believe what I have written today, I deserve very little of the credit. I know that my words are doing nothing but reminding them of the truth and wisdom that already lies inherent within them, awaiting recognition and activation. Someone once said that there is no such thing as an original thought. There is more truth to that than we may know. So, unlike Emerson, I don't hate quotations, and I shall continue to use them. Likewise, I encourage you to do the same. Just remember, it's not the words that you are really trying to convey but rather what they mean in your heart. You can quote me on that!

Mindfulness Practice

⮞ Pick up your favorite book and read a passage that truly speaks to your heart.

⮞ Take a pen and paper and write down what those words mean to you, using your own words.

⮞ Notice how the quote has simply awakened that place within you where the "yes" lives, that place in you that already knows the meaning behind the words, even before you read them.

⮞ Now share your understanding of that quote with another person and marvel in the process of divine sublimation: ideas moving as energy between individuals, seeking the "yes."

97

IT'S ALL ABOUT RELATIONSHIPS

When the body sinks into death, the essence of man is revealed. Man is a knot, a web, a mesh into which relationships are tied. Only those relationships matter. The body is an old crock that nobody will miss. I have never known a man to think of himself when dying. Never.

~Antoine De Saint-Exupery

One of the things I like best about being a minister is that I have the honor of performing sacred ceremonies such as christenings, memorial services, and weddings. As odd as it may seem, all of these events have something very much in common. They are all about relationships and friendships. Christenings allow us to celebrate the beginning of a relationship yet to be between oneself, a child, and God. A memorial service allows us to honor and celebrate the relationship and friendship we have shared with a loved one over a period of time. A wedding ceremony (or commitment ceremony) allows us to honor and celebrate the deepening of our awareness of love's presence between two individuals. This is when two people have the opportunity to become true best friends and life partners. I cherish watching how that invisible spirit of love is made so visible in the gaze between two people who can see past the physical trappings of the body as they look into one another, connecting as one in that divine essence that permeates the entire beings of both. From a spiritual perspective, we have come here to have relationships. Relationships are the vessels in which we travel toward a common destination, which is a greater realization of unconditional love. From the cradle to the grave and all along the way in between, it is the relationships we have that really make life worth living. From the depths of our most cherished relationships come our friendships—those people with whom we want to spend time. Can you imagine going through life with all the accoutrements and material things you could desire except for the ability to be with other people, especially the ones you love most deeply? The whole journey would be meaningless! Truly, when it is all said and done, only relationships matter.

Mindfulness Practice	
	Perhaps this is the day when you can stop and consider all the people in your life who mean the most to you.
	Now call them or write them and tell them so. Reach out and touch another life, for your sake . . . and theirs.
	Finally, put it on your agenda to establish one new friendship this week.

98

UNCONDITIONAL LOVE: THE ULTIMATE SYMPHONY

What is a loving heart? A loving heart is sensitive to the whole of life, to all persons; a loving heart doesn't harden itself to any person or thing.

~Anthony De Mellow

Recently, I received a request to address the concept of unconditional love. With an upcoming family event, a woman stated that she would be required to spend some time around certain family members who she had a serious problem liking, let alone loving. This is not an issue uncommon to most of us. As metaphysicians, we are often confronted with issues and ideas that challenge our ideals and core values. Unconditional love is certainly one of those issues. From a spiritual perspective, we know that God is all there is. We also know that God is the essence of unconditional love because It gives Itself freely to all of Its creation, with no strings attached. To do otherwise would be for God to literally reject a part of Itself and withhold love from Itself, which is a divine impossibility. Imagine that you are at a classical musical concert and because of a bad experience with French horns you had at some point in your history, you made up your mind that you can't stand the sight or sound of them. So, you have determined to try and block out any music that comes from the French horn section. In the process of doing this, however, you also miss the incredible performance of the flutes and piano . . . the entire symphony! Life is like a symphony: You can't resist one part of the performance and enjoy the rest of it. At some point, we must reconcile the personal issues that cause us to feel separated from others if we are to enter into a deeper understanding of what unconditional love is. Until we can gaze deeply enough into life to see the whole, irrespective of our attachments to the parts, unconditional love will be only a theory that dances around in our heads as impractical and impossible. The sad part is, there will be a piece (peace) missing within because we have rejected some part of God's presence. Until we can embrace the whole, we can't really draw the full meaning from the experience called the human life. I do believe it is possible to love someone unconditionally and at the same time be clear that you don't like being around them. Unconditional love doesn't mean unconditional acceptance of a person or their actions. It doesn't mean that you are a doormat to be walked on. It means that you are not attached to excluding them from your opportunity (obligation) to be a fully developed expression of God's love for Its self. You can love the presence of God within all people without having warm fuzzies for everyone. (Yes, it's there whether they know it or act like it or not.) Just keep reminding yourself that you are loving God, not a personality attached to some point in your history. In doing so, you give yourself a chance to enjoy the entire symphony of life, and since you are the conductor, you should enjoy the whole concert!

Mindfulness Practice

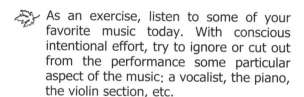 As an exercise, listen to some of your favorite music today. With conscious intentional effort, try to ignore or cut out from the performance some particular aspect of the music: a vocalist, the piano, the violin section, etc.

Notice how much less you enjoy the performance.

If you want to extend this exercise into "real life," think of that "special" person (or people) you have decided to exclude from your list of those you love unconditionally. Throughout this day, keep focusing on how much you don't unconditionally love them.

At the end of the day, become aware of how many other opportunities you had to love today but missed because of your attachment to not loving. Love the whole of life everyday and be grateful that you have the awareness to do so.

99   THE BEST VISION COMES FROM THE "INNER I"

Where there is no vision, the people perish.

~Proverbs 29:18

To come to be you must have a vision of Being, a Dream, a Purpose, and a Principle. You will become what your vision is.

~Peter Nivio Zarlenga

Vision is not only that which comes from using our physical eyes but also our hearts and minds together. It's using the "inner I" to see the possibilities for something wonderful before it is ever manifest. A vision is something that every person, family, business, and organization needs. It moves us forward and determines where we are going, and perhaps more important, it determines what we stand for, it clarifies our purpose for being. Many people are so busy just doing life, getting by day to day that they never realize the deeper purpose and meaning of life itself. So, they wander aimlessly from day to day. As days turn into years, at the end of their journey here, they look back and think, "That's it? Where was the juice and sweetness and meaning of being here?" Without a vision, our life's journey can seem more or less meaningless. We blow about like a sailboat on the ocean without a rudder or compass—we get nowhere fast. If we are not committed to navigating our lives with vision, any current–moment trauma drama will pull us off course and we lose sight of the shoreline, our goals and destination, our reason and purpose for being. Conversely, as we clarify our vision, our lives take on a direction and dimension we haven't seen before. True visionaries are far and few between. Why?

Because it requires a willingness to go where we have not gone before; that's where the juice, passion, meaning . . . and uncertainty are. It requires a willingness to declare a course and stay it, irrespective of the sailing conditions, which blow others off course so easily.

Do you have a vision for your life? If you don't, it is never too late to realize it and develop one. What are some of the qualities of a true vision? Our vision has to take us someplace that invites us to grow and become part of something larger than we currently are. As spiritually grounded individuals, this means we must also remember to make room for God in our vision. A true vision serves other people in some beneficial way. It requires that we step into the vision with a deep and unshakeable faith, knowing that as a result of manifesting a purpose-driven life, when we leave this planet, it is a better place than it was when we arrived. Our vision will also call us to use our most natural talents. Finally, declaring our vision will require that we fully embrace it. Words alone are insufficient. To make our vision our reality requires definite action, some of which may cause a few new stretch marks. Stretch marks are caused by growth. This is why there are so few true visionary leaders and so many followers: It's a lot easier to watch someone else do the growing! A visionary must be not only open to but in constant search of growth. There is no growth at the center of our comfort zone—we have to come to the edge and lean over a bit, into the unknown. So, my question for the day is, What is your vision for your life? What do you stand for? Are you willing to grow into that vision? Begin to use your "inner I" and you will see the possibilities of a life you have never known before.

Mindfulness
Practice

➣ Try to access your heart space today and explore what may be lying there, awaiting your recognition.

➣ Is there a passion to create something that is life affirming and adds expanse, joy, balance, peace, healing, growth, and love to your life, as well as others? Your vision will find its roots in purpose and meaning.

➣ What gives you a sense of purpose? Are you willing to declare it to the world?

➣ If you are, describe it by writing it down as a statement of purpose, a vision statement. Try to keep it to no more than ten to twelve words at the most. (As an example, my personal vision and our church's vision are one and the same: "Expanding the awareness of God's presence in all.")

➣ Listen more to your heart and less to your head and see what shows up when you use your "inner I."

100   AS WITHIN...

Our world is in crisis because of our perception;
how we see the world creates the world in which we
live. Ultimately, it's about each one of us taking the
responsibility for being the Presence of God.

~Walter Starcke

I have a question for you: When you woke up this morning, in those very first few moments, what was your perception of life? What were the first thoughts that came to you? Did you think about the workday that lay ahead and all you had to do? Did you think about a problem you went to bed with last night that still hadn't been resolved? Did you fret about various world events? Did you think about the economy and your investment portfolio? Did you think about how badly someone recently treated you? Did you think about just rolling over and going back to sleep? On the other hand, did you think about the amazing gifts that this day brings with it? Did you think about the blessings that surround you? Did you appreciate your ability to choose to enter into this day with the simple awareness that you are a living, breathing, walking, talking incarnation of God? That's quite a contrast, isn't it? Perception is everything.

It's my belief that you and I are living manifestations of God whether we know it or not. As we open ourselves to having a shift in our perception of this truth and how it manifests in our lives, it can literally change our world. I especially like the above quote from Walter Starcke, because it so clearly points to a universal principle: How we choose to see the world determines our experience of it. As within, so without. When we perceive the world through our human eyes, we often tend to focus on the terror, the lack and limitation, and the fear of what tomorrow might bring. That's because the predominant energy of the collective consciousness is stuck in the human condition, which today is in great turmoil. When the human condition becomes our reality and point of perception, by the universal law of cause and effect, it must become our experience. The good news is that it doesn't have to be that way because we have a choice. The alternative is for each of us to choose a different perception by taking responsibility for our beliefs and thoughts, which manifest as our reality. I know that most of us are quite aware of this premise already. However, a little reminder once in a while can't hurt any of us and may help us all. Let's face it, it's real easy to let ourselves get caught up in the drama that is playing before us on the world stage. We often forget we are far more than just participants or victims playing an unconscious role in the drama.

So, tomorrow morning and every morning thereafter, I invite you to start with a prayer of thankfulness. When you first open your eyes, take a moment and make a conscious choice to make space between every thought and every breath for God's presence to be felt and realized. Ask yourself, "How can I be present today?" Do this one simple thing and you will be amazed how it changes your world, one day at a time. How will God show up today in the world by means of you?

Mindfulness Practice

- Take a quick scan of your mind right now. What is your perception of your life and the world today at this very moment?

- Can you make space between your thoughts and breaths for God's presence to be revealed? Nod your head saying, "Yes, of course I can." Now, the only question is, will you?

- Remember, as within . . .

101

---

*Sooner or later every one of us breathes an atom that
has been breathed by anyone you can think of who has
lived before us — Michelangelo or George Washington
or Moses.*

~Jacob Bronowski

One day, many many years ago, great contributors to humankind
such as Mozart, Leonardo da Vinci, Plato, and Socrates as well as
spiritual masters such as Jesus, Buddha, and Saint Francis stood and
gazed up at the same moon at which we often gaze. I wonder what
thoughts ran through their minds regarding their purpose here, their
time here, and their connection with the universe. As you take your
next breath, imagine that you are sharing sacred space with those
people who came before you and made a difference. In so many ways,
they contributed to who you are and what you have today. Now,
imagine that you are breathing the same atoms that those individuals
breathed. Feel their presence and personalize the gifts they brought to
humanity. Finally, realize that you too shall pass those atoms on to
some other person who will live thousands of years from now. There is
even more you shall add: Imagine the gifts you have yet to bring to
humanity. Imagine those people two thousand years from now,
imagining you. What is the gift you will give to them?

This kind of a visualization exercise puts life into a new
perspective, doesn't it? Life really is a sacred continuum where
everything touches at some point. Of course, that "point" is not
subject to time or matter because it is all energy in motion, and in
truth, it is all happening in the now. Think about it: The ideas that
moved through Leonardo da Vinci's mind became the templates for

inventions yet to be given form, many of which we enjoy today. Jesus and Buddha realized that the universe was interconnected and that we all share the same common ground: infinite life. Nothing changes but form. Essentially, we are all one—always have been, always will be. The profound implication of this idea is compelling to contemplate; what affects one of us, affects us all for eternity. So, make no mistake about it, what you believe, think, and do today will touch those yet to come. My question for you to ponder is this: What will your legacy to the future "now" be? When we live each moment in an awareness that we are—right here and now—adding something to the universal whole, I know we will be more mindful of our thoughts, deeds, and actions, yes? Isn't this life an amazing trip?

Mindfulness Practice

- ☞ Take time to go outdoors tonight and simply stare out into space. Observe the moon and stars and breathe deeply.

- ☞ Contemplate your unity with the infinite. Feel a sense of wonder in the fact that only a cosmic heartbeat has passed since Jesus, Buddha, and other ancient masters did the very same thing.

- ☞ Feel the connectedness of life and ask yourself, "What shall I add to this amazing sacred continuum with how I live today?"

- ☞ Be mindful—you do make a difference.

RECOMMENDED READING

Bach, Richard. (1977). *Illusions*. Delacorte Press.

Butterworth, Eric. (1983). *Spiritual economics*. Unity Village, MO: Unity School of Christianity.

Carter-Scott, Cherie. (1998). *If life is a game, these are the rules*. New York: Broadway Books.

Chopra, Deepak. (1994). *The seven spiritual laws of success*. New York: Amber-Allen.

De Mellow, Anthony. (1990). *Awareness*. New York: Doubleday.

De Mellow, Anthony. (1991). *The way to love*. New York: Doubleday.

Gibran, Kahlil. (1977). *The prophet*. New York: Alfred Knopf.

Hanh, Thich Nhat. (1998). *The heart of the Buddha's teaching*. New York: Broadway Books.

Harbula, Patrick. (2003). *The magic of the soul*. Thousand Oaks, CA: Peak Publications.

Holmes, Ernest. (1938). *The science of mind*. New York: G.P. Putnam's Sons.

Huber, Cheri. (2000). *Suffering is optional*. Murphys, CA: Keep It Simple Books.

Jampolsky, Gerald. (1979). *Love is letting go of fear*. Berkeley, CA: Celestial Arts.

Jones, Dennis Merritt. (1999). *How to speak Religious Science*. Camarillo, CA: DeVorss.

Kabat-Zinn, Jon. (1994). *Wherever you go, there you are*. New York: Hyperion.

Kornfield, Jack. (2000). *After the ecstasy, the laundry*. New York: Bantam Books.

Kornfield, Jack. (2002). *The art of forgiveness, lovingkindness and peace*. New York: Bantam Books.

McGraw, Phillip C. (2001). *Self matters*. New York: Simon & Schuster Source.

Morrissey, Mary Manin. (1996). *Building your field of dreams*. New York: Bantam Books.

Morrissey, Mary Manin. (2001). *No less than greatness*. New York: Bantam Books.

Moses, Harry Morgan. (1999). *It's easy when you know how*. San Diego, CA: NTC Press.

Muktananda, Swami. (1994). *Where are you going?* South Fallsburg, N.Y: SYDA Foundation.

Muller, Wayne. (1996). *How, then, shall we live?* New York: Bantam Books.

Myss, Carolyn. (1996). *Anatomy of the spirit*. New York: Harmony Books.

Nepo, Mark. (2000). *The book of awakening*. Berkeley, CA: Conari Press.

Paul, Jordan. (2003). *Becoming your own hero*. Seattle, WA: Hara Publishing.

Peck, M. Scott. (1997). *The different drum*. New York: Touchstone Books.

Prakashananda, Swami. (1994). *Don't think of a monkey*. Freemont, CA: Sarasvati Productions.

Price, John Randolph. (2001). *Removing the masks that bind us*. Carlsbad, CA: Hay House.

Reynolds, Caroline. (2001). *Spiritual fitness*. Hammersmith, London: Thorsons/Imprint of HarperCollins.

Ruiz, Don Miguel. (1997). *The four agreements*. San Rafael, CA: Amber-Allen.

Sorensen, Stephanie. (1996). *Unlimited visibility*. Camarillo, CA: DeVorss.

Sorensen, Stephanie. (2000). *The sacred continuum*. Camarillo, CA: DeVorss.

Starcke, Walter. (1988). *Homesick for heaven*. Boerne, TX: The Guadalupe Press.

/>

Starcke, Walter. (1998). *It's all God*. Boerne, TX: The Guadalupe Press.

Tolle, Eckhart. (1999). *The power of now*. Navato, CA: New World Library.

Zukav, Gary. (1989). *The seat of the soul*. New York: Fireside.

Zukav, Gary, and Linda Francis. (2001). *The heart of the soul*. New York: Simon & Schuster.

ABOUT THE AUTHOR

Having been a motivational force in New Thought for more than twenty years, Dennis Merritt Jones, D.D. has often been referred to as "a teacher's teacher." In 1985, he founded the Simi Valley Center for Positive Living in Southern California where the vision to "Expand the Awareness of God's Presence in All" continues under his leadership as senior minister and director. With his wife Diane, they share a nearby home fifty miles west of Los Angeles.

"Dr. D," as his spiritual community calls him, believes everyone has the capacity and responsibility to contribute something positive to this world, leaving it a better place than it was when they arrived. To this end, he believes New Thought will be among the fastest growing teachings in the years to come because it offers a realistic approach to life in the 21st century with a contemporary, life-affirming, and spiritually logical and positive outlook. Dr. Jones states, "A positive thinker grounded in his or her spirituality is the most powerful person on the face of the planet."

CONTACT INFORMATION

To order this book, please visit www.DennisMerrittJones.com. For information regarding Dr. Jones' availability for seminars, personal coaching, retreats, and keynote speaking engagements, or for information regarding this book or other books and classes available on tape and CD by Dr. Jones, please visit www.DennisMerrittJones.com or write to P.O. Box 940837, Simi Valley, CA 93094-0837.

COMING SOON!

Watch for *The Art of Being: 101* More *Ways to Practice Purpose in Your Life*.